A Century's Child

The Story of

Thompson Children's Home

1886-1986

BARBARA B. LOCKMAN

Published by
Thompson Children's Home
Charlotte, North Carolina

ISBN 0-912081-02-3
Library of Congress Catalog Card Number 85-52345

For Arden and Philip

Acknowledgments

No project of this scope is ever undertaken, or accomplished, without the help, support and guidance of many individuals. The author gratefully acknowledges all those who contributed to the completion of this history and in particular:

Brenda Lea, John Powell, Stern Dixon, and the entire staff of Thompson Children's Home for opening their records and supplying information, answers, resources, and support throughout this 14-month project;

James O. Moore, Haywood Smith, John Powell and Richard Urquhart, members of the 1986 Centennial Committee, for reviewing each chapter and offering valuable insights and suggestions for revision;

Michelle Francis, archivist at the Diocesan House in Raleigh for her invaluable assistance and genuine interest in the book;

George Powell, Mary Froebe, Stella Henson, Ben Nash and Kenneth Thomas, alumni of The Thompson Orphanage, and Lillie Mae White, former employee, for freely sharing their experiences;

Edith Louise Liner for laying the groundwork in her 1976 history of The Thompson Orphanage;

the staff of the North Carolina Room of the Charlotte-Mecklenburg Library for answering every inquiry with patience and enthusiasm;

Elizabeth Reid Murray, author of *Wake: Capital County of North Carolina,* for sharing her methods of research;

Beth Kreutzer, Mary Canfield and Dorothy Lockman for seeing that my children were not orphaned during the writing of this book;

Earl and Elizabeth Borneman for providing that parental love and example every child craves;

and last but far from least, Jim Lockman, without whose steadfast understanding, encouragement, love, support and prayers, this history would never have been completed.

In Dedication to
James Osborne Moore

Few people are able to integrate the past with the present and then anticipate the future. Even more rare is the individual who for over fifty years can offer such an ability to an organization.

James Osborne Moore is such a rare person. His roots extend to Thompson's beginning as the first superintendent, the Reverend Edwin A. Osborne, was his great-uncle. James Moore was reared in a loving and caring family, but he felt the tragedy of death as a boy and young man. His mother died when he was nine years old and his father died during his sixteenth year. These losses made him constantly sensitive to the plight of Thompson's children.

After graduating from the University of North Carolina's School of Law, he and his wife, Jane Morrison Moore, settled in Charlotte. Beginning a new practice and rearing children amid the economic struggles of the Great Depression would for many foreclose the possibility of volunteer service, but in 1934 James Moore began functioning as Thompson's attorney, a role he has continued for over fifty years — never charging for his services.

As a Board member, he recognized that orphans were diminishing in numbers. He led an important planning committee in 1959 that foresaw the need for specialized care of troubled children. His committee came to see that not only the children of broken and troubled homes needed care, but the entire family system must be helped. Such concepts were ahead of conventional practice; however we were blessed to have Board members with the vision of James Moore.

Presently, James Moore serves on another Thompson Long-Range Planning Committee. His vision of the future is still keen, and he continues to challenge Thompson to good stewardship. He believes that Thompson should appreciate its heritage so that the past helps guide the future, but he also advises that we look ahead. He continues to challenge Thompson to have the courage to adapt the agency's mission to the needs of the future.

James Moore's life is closely linked to his religious faith. He on many occasions advised prayers for God's guidance when Thompson faced difficult problems. For over fifty years he has helped Thompson to serve over a thousand needy and troubled children. In thankfulness for his faith, leadership and vision, this history of Thompson Orphanage is dedicated to the honor of James Osborne Moore.

Foreword

Often the general public imagines church agencies to be rigid, intractable institutions. Some naively believe that church-related children's homes are especially self-serving, desiring to maintain a cloistered, unnatural existence for children.

A careful reading of the history of Thompson Orphanage and Training Institution explodes such myths. Mrs. Lockman has made an important contribution to both the long-standing Episcopalian who remembers from early-childhood Thompson Orphanage's Thanksgiving mite boxes and to the reader who has been introduced to Thompson Children's Home in more recent years. She has discovered the romance of Thompson from the dusty files of Board minutes, superintendent's reports, letters and personal recollections. Perhaps her most important revelation is that Thompson's history is replete with courage and daring as those called to its mission have sought to serve the most pressing needs of children amid unfavorable climates.

The early founders without promise of continuing funds risked themselves to serve the orphans of North Carolina in the late 1800s. After enduring several economic depressions, two World Wars, the Korean War, the Vietnam War, and the advent of the Nuclear Age, the spirit of Thompson Children's Home is still strong. Thompson's services are now centered upon rehabilitation and treatment of emotionally-disturbed children and their families. Yet, the author's central message is that a church children's home is far more than buildings, an endowment or an established way of operating. Its vision must be a call to mission. This mission requires continuous re-evaluation and re-dedication.

The course of Thompson's ministry in its next century is uncertain. However, a review of its first hundred years shows that men and women have come forth to discover God's will for this special ministry at critical times of change and progress.

What Mrs. Lockman portrays is not dull history, but a pilgrimmage of faith and hope in a loving God. If we will but follow the example of our founders, some future author will likely record Thompson's history in 2086 as the agency prepares for its third century of caring.

John Y. Powell, Ph.D.
Executive Director

Portions of this history, set in italics, depict created scenes relating to the history of The Thompson Orphanage and Training Institution. They are based on sound historical evidence and are included for the reader's enjoyment and increased understanding of the events and individuals shaping the story of the statewide child caring agency known today as Thompson Children's Home.

"I will not leave you as orphans."
John 14: 18

Chapter I

A Dream Takes Root

1850-1886

Edwin Osborne again raised his sleeve to catch a rivulet of sweat before it could plunge down the threads of his long mustache. He stood by the window watching as several small children dropped sewing pins into the deep cracks left in the dried summer clay along West Trade Street. It was a great game, wondering if those pins would tumble their way to China.[1]

It was for children much like these that Osborne and the others were gathered in John Wilkes' parlor this sultry August morning. Listening to their rising laughter, Osborne was overtaken by the memory of more somber, silent children who year after year stood before the orphan's court in counties across the state. He had watched their rigid faces and darting eyes, waiting, as if in anticipation of a sentence, for intoned pronouncements which would determine their future: an assignment to apprenticeship, appointment of a guardian, and the disposition of their property. As a lawyer, Osborne knew well the laws concerning homeless and destitute children; as a priest, he felt an overwhelming responsibility. Now, finally, there was to be an alternative to the county poorhouse and to indentured

labor for children. The long-held dream was materializing before his eyes.

Osborne left the youngsters to their carefree games and joined the others seated around the parlor in the practical business of organizing and operating a home for orphaned and destitute children under the name of The Thompson Orphanage and Training Institution.

He took his seat as the Rt. Rev. Theodore B. Lyman opened the meeting with a roll call of the newly-appointed Board of Managers present: the Rev. William R. Wetmore, James F. Payne, Capt. Baxter H. Moore, and Edwin A. Osborne, who, serving as secretary pro-tem, began his note-taking with the heading "August 10, 1886."

The origin of the dream which became the Thompson Orphanage and Training Institution goes back well beyond the first official meeting of the Board of Managers, held at the Charlotte home of St. Peter's Church vestryman John Wilkes on August 10, 1886. Its roots coil and twine through the social and political fabric of North Carolina and the growth and resources of the Episcopal church, uniquely joining together the tenacity and compassion of a Confederate officer, the lofty vision of a New England educator, and the benevolence of a Bertie County plantation owner's widow.

If there is a definable beginning to the dream, it may be in the decision made between 1849 and 1850 by Benjamin Swan Bronson to leave his native Maine to teach the classics in North Carolina where, it was estimated, more than half of the population was illiterate.[2] A graduate of Yale, Benjamin Bronson quickly established a reputation as a teacher of considerable ability and scholarship particularly among the prominent plantation-owning families in the counties of Hertford and Bertie where he had settled. These were families for whom formal education was prized, and who possessed the financial resources necessary to privately school their children. There was no provision in North Carolina for public education, the prevailing philosophy being that education was a private, not a public matter.[3]

Benjamin Bronson's original religious affili-

Benjamin Swan Bronson

ation is unknown, although while continuing to teach in Hertford, he studied divinity under Alfred A. Watson, rector of the Church of The Advent in Williamston, and on May 21, 1854 was ordained a deacon in the Episcopal church. Three years later he became a priest in ceremonies at St. Luke's Church, Salisbury. He entered the priesthood at a time when Bishop Thomas Atkinson was fervently seeking to enlarge the church's membership following former Bishop Levi Ives' disavowal of Episcopal doctrine in favor of the Roman Catholic Church. Part of the church's appeal to Benjamin Bronson may have been its respect for education:

> Avoiding revivals, camp meetings and emotional devices, esteeming formal services and an educated ministry, appealing to the more aristocratic, educated, and wealthy people in the towns and the plantation East, the Episcopal Church possessed wealth and influence . . . [4]

Almost immediately after becoming a deacon, Bronson was sent to St. Thomas Church, Windsor, where he served from 1854 to 1860. He simultaneously served Grace Church established in 1854 in nearby Woodville, from September 17, 1854 to August 25, 1860, spending these early years of his ministry in the counties where he had been revered as a teacher. Among his friends and parishioners were some of the most eminent people of the region, including state legislator and plantation owner Lewis Thompson, one of the five founding vestrymen and trustees of Grace Church.

THE THOMPSONS OF BERTIE

Lewis Thompson was an influential, highly respected figure in the Upper South, "a man of correct taste, of a thorough sense of propriety, of ripe judgement and great energy of character."[5] A 1827 graduate of the University of North Carolina, he represented Bertie County as a member of the House of Commons in 1831 and 1840 and as a senator in 1844 and 1848, indicative not only of his statesmanship but of his considerable wealth. Qualifications for holding office in North Carolina required ownership of at least one hundred acres for a member of the House of Commons, three hundred acres for state senator.[6] In addition to vast land holdings in Bertie County which produced cotton and grain, Thompson owned and managed a 5,000 acre cotton and sugar plantation at Lecompte, in Rapides Parish, Louisiana, which in 1850 was valued at $252,281.[7]

Thompson's family included his wife Margaret Clark, whose benevolence was recognized as "the leading and marked characteristic of her life,"[8] and their children Thomas W., Mary Bond, Martha Clark ("Pattie"), and William Clark.

Following their private education at home, Thompson's daughters were sent in 1860 to St. Mary's School in Raleigh. One of Mary Thompson's first letters home affirms the value of their earlier education:

> Dr. Smedes said our examination give [sic] credit to us and our teachers. He put us in separate classes and with some girls larger than ourselves, and I am so much obliged to you for sending us to school so long at home and having such good teachers.[9]

The regular flow of letters from the girls and from William Thompson, managing his father's interests in Louisiana, contained frequent inquiries about Grace Church priest and family friend, Benjamin Bronson who, just before the outbreak of the Civil War, accepted a call from Christ Church in St. Michael's, Maryland. While in Maryland, Bronson maintained a relationship through correspondence with Lewis Thompson, both personal and business.

Still deeply attached to the people and to the Diocese of North Carolina, Benjamin Bronson returned during "the dark days of 1865 and 1866"[10] to North Carolina. In 1867 he was assigned to Charlotte as rector of St. Peter's Church, embarking on a path which was to lead directly to the formation of the Thompson Orphanage.

POST-WAR CHARLOTTE

Bronson was known as a man of "strong faith, clear vision, and high and inspiring ideals, a devoted advocate of education and institutional Church work."[11] Joseph Blount Chesire, Jr., a successor at St. Peter's and later Bishop of the Diocese of North Carolina, repeatedly admitted that "the course of development of our church work and church life was . . . more influenced by

Lewis Thompson

him than by any other man who has held the position."[12]

When Bronson came to Charlotte in 1867, he found the town bruised but not beaten. It had been peacefully occupied by Federal troops in 1865, some of whom still remained. Many of the industries which had thrived during the War, manufacturing food, clothing and other supplies for the Confederacy, continued to flourish, easing Charlotte's economic recovery. A building boom was already on, adding 12 new stores and 75 other buildings during the first six months of 1867.[13]

Among the new rector's congregation were many of Charlotte's distinguished citizens, including Col. W. R. Myers whose thousand-acre cotton farm overlooked Charlotte to the southeast, and Capt. John Wilkes, senior warden and head of the vestry. It was John Wilkes who, along with former St. Peter's rector George M. Everhart, had formed and operated the Protestant Episcopal Church Publishing Association during the War to print and distribute religious materials to Confederate soldiers and to publish *The Church Intelligencer*.[14]

Wilkes had also been the instigator of a plan involving the state's Episcopal churches in a successful blockade-running escapade in 1863. Under his direction, six North Carolina parishes contributed funds for the purchase of five bales of cotton, shipped on the "S.S. Cornubia" and sold in England to purchase Bibles and a special edition of the Prayer Book of the Confederate States.[15] These Prayer Books were the only ones brought safely through the blockade to Wilmington. Other editions of a Confederate Prayer Book ordered by the Episcopal churches in the South never made it, being instead tossed overboard or sold at prize auctions in the North.

The devastating aftermath of the War, which left most of North Carolina "divided, defeated, and exhausted."[16] was less apparent in Charlotte. But while making heroes of many of the town's citizens and stimulating its economic growth, the War had stifled educational opportunities. Benjamin Bronson, convinced that the role of the church should extend far beyond its physical walls and into the community, quickly fired his vestry with the idea of building and operating a boys' school in Charlotte.

ST. PETER'S SCHOOL

In a letter to Lewis Thompson posted in Charlotte and dated April 23 (presumably 1867), Benjamin Bronson expressed his intention of attending "the Convention in Education" and added, "I am very anxious to meet you there. In fact I doubt whether I should go were it not for the hope of meeting you."[17] Lewis Thompson was a member of the Constitutional Convention meeting in Raleigh.[18] It is assumed that Bronson must have discussed with Lewis Thompson at this time his desire to open a boys' school in Charlotte.

On August 2, 1867, as recorded in the land records of Mecklenburg County, "John Wilkes and others(s), Wardens and Vestrymen of St. Peter's Church" purchased approximately 21 acres of land outside the city limits along Sugar Creek from Benjamin Morrow for $520. Its boundaries ran from "the great road on the bank of Little Sugar Creek" following the "meandering of said creek about twenty-one poles to a large stone at the mouth of a ditch," on to another ditch at Cedar Street, a stake "in the Providence Road," and finally back to Sugar Creek.[19] Here the St. Peter's School was to be established.

Charlotte had few other schools in operation at the time. Rev. R. H. Griffith and Armistead Burwell had taught a boys' school since 1865, and Rev. A. G. Stacy and his faculty were conducting classes for the Mecklenburg Female College, set up in the old Military Institute.[20] Students were also enrolled in Biddle Institute and the Charlotte Female Institute.

As Bronson struggled to raise funds for operating St. Peter's School, he received news from Bertie County of the deaths in November, 1867, of 18-year old Pattie Thompson and of her father Lewis Thompson on December 9, 1867. Thompson's death at age 59 may have robbed him of a more prominent place in national history. An item in Charlotte's *The Western Democrat* dated December 17, 1867, expressed the views of the newspaper's Raleigh correspondent concerning Thompson's political potential:

> It is regarded as settled among the Republicans that the 'inevitable smoker,' U.S. Grant is to be the Republican candidate for President. It is thought the candidate for Vice-President will be given to some Southern State. In connection with this, the name of Hon. Lewis Thompson of Bertie has been spoken of. In my opinion, there is no better man for the position in the Union. Mr. Thompson's ability is second to no man now spoken of for President or Vice President. He is a pure man — one who would dignify and elevate the office of Speaker of United States Senate.[21]

News of Thompson's death had apparently not reached the correspondent before the story was printed.

The cause of Pattie Thompson's death is not documented, nor is that of her father's, although there is speculation that Lewis Thompson's death was hastened by grief, as indicated in a tribute by members of the Bertie County Court in February, 1868:

> Strong man as he was, nature had full play in his heart. His life was doubtless hastened to its close by grief for the death of a lovely daughter. His sympathies were ever with his friends in their bereavements, and his firm

manhood gave way when death took from his household the child of his love.[22]

At the time of his death, Lewis Thompson was chairman of the Bertie County Court.

In memory of her daughter and husband, Margaret Clark Thompson gave a considerable sum of money, estimated by various accounts to have ranged between $2,000 — $5,000, to Benjamin Bronson for use in establishing the St. Peter's School in Charlotte.

With these funds and other contributions gathered through visits to "distant parts of the State and country,"[24] Bronson purchased additional land adjacent to that held by the vestry, including 57 acres on March 6, 1869 and 182 acres on December 20, 1869 from W.B. and Hassie Thomas.[25] The deeds were registered and signed by Edwin A. Osborne, Clerk of Superior Court in Mecklenburg County, who later played the guiding role in the establishment of the Thompson Orphanage.

THE THOMPSON INSTITUTE

With determined hands, Benjamin Bronson began to construct a school building on the property, scooping out the clay from the banks of Sugar Creek, forming and burning it into brick.[26] In gratitude to the Thompson family, he renamed the school the Thompson Institute and called the classroom building Thompson Hall.

Bronson taught the school by himself for several terms, later adding the assistance of the Rev. Lucien Holmes.[27] In 1872 he began preparations for expanding the scope of the school to include the entire diocese, hoping to convey all property, whether owned personally or by the vestry, to a board of trustees for the Thompson Institute.[28] These plans never materialized.

Though a man of lofty vision, determination and enthusiasm, Benjamin Bronson lacked the administrative skills necessary to carry out his ideas. The vestry appears to have taken no part in the school after 1872 and by the following year the Thompson Institute was closed.

The property lay deserted for many years except for the occasional digging of clay with which to make brick. In 1878, the St. Peter's Hospital, organized by Bronson and his church, moved to Poplar and West Sixth Streets in Charlotte, occupying a new brick building made from clay dug at the overgrown plot of ground people now called "the old Bronson place."[30]

A PRESBYTERIAN COMES TO ST. PETER'S

Prior to the closing of the Thompson Institute, sometime between 1869 and 1870, Benjamin Bronson officiated at the baptism of Mary Lloyd and Alexander Duncan Moore Osborne and the confirmation by Bishop Thomas B. Atkinson of the children's father, Edwin Augustus Osborne. Recognized as a Confederate hero, Osborne was a Presbyterian who had not given the matter of church membership much thought until his marriage to an Episcopalian, Frances Swan Moore, and the birth of their children. He admitted in his autobiography:

> Not knowing anything of the Episcopal Church and thinking it made little difference about which 'church' one was a member of, I naturally thought my wife would unite with me in my membership as a Presbyterian. But I soon discovered that this was an utter mistake and there was no probability that she would ever change her membership into another body of Christians. This put me to thinking and to reading, and I soon became reconciled to the idea of having our two children baptized in the Church. The more I looked into the matter . . . the more I became persuaded of the correctness of the claims of the Episcopal Church to be a true branch of the Holy Catholic Church, and soon made my decision to be confirmed, and soon afterwards I decided to become a candidate for Holy Orders in the Church.[31]

Following his confirmation, he began to study for the ministry under Benjamin Bronson and was ordained deacon in St. Peter's Church on June 3, 1877. Though he had already resigned his position as Clerk of Superior Court in Mecklenburg County, he still hoped to continue his practice of law. However, he was sent immediately to Calvary Parish in the mountain town of Fletcher where his days were totally absorbed in mission work. He traveled and preached often at Bat Cave, Rutherfordton, Chimney Rock, Hendersonville, Bowman's Bluff, and built a little church called Mount Calvary near Burnette Cove.

On May 22, 1881, in a ceremony in Christ

Church, Raleigh, Col. Edwin A. Osborne was ordained a priest in the Episcopal church.

THE WINDS OF CHANGE

While Edwin Osborne plodded on horseback through the North Carolina mountains, things were changing rapidly at the parish of St. Peter's in Charlotte. The Rev. Benjamin Bronson resigned at the end of 1878 and in 1879 accepted a call to St. Timothy's Church in Wilson. In each of the next three years, there was a different rector at St. Peter's. Then in the Spring of 1881, Joseph Blount Cheshire, Jr. was called by Bishop Lyman to the Charlotte parish. Many of his friends dispaired over the assignment, calling St. Peter's "one of the hardest and most undesirable parishes in the Diocese."[32]

Cheshire found, instead, a receptive congregation, eager for the missionary projects he proposed. One of those was the organization in 1884 of St. Mark's mission in the Long Creek community of Mecklenburg County. He began preaching at the community's Beech Cliff School House on November 18, 1883, continuing weekly services there through the summer of the following year, building up a loyal congregation of mostly former Presbyterians.[33]

To assist with the growth of the mission, Cheshire turned to another former Presbyterian, Edwin Osborne, asking him to preach at St. Mark's August 12-17, 1884. Osborne recorded in his autobiography:

> This was a complete surprise to me. I had but a slight acquaintance with Mr. Cheshire, and had never preached a mission, and did not want to leave home at that time. But the meeting had been appointed for that week and the call was most urgent.[34]

So great was his reception in Long Creek that by the third evening the small schoolhouse was filled to overflowing. Cheshire later remarked that "the preaching of the Rev. Mr. Osborne . . . was the greatest element, humanly speaking, in the interest and success of those meetings."[35] At Bishop Theodore Lyman's request, Osborne took charge of the mission, returning to Charlotte in January, 1885, and settling his family in the same house on North Graham Street they had left over seven years earlier.[36]

Edwin Osborne's monetary support was

Edwin Augustus Osborne

"meager", but, as Joseph Cheshire recalled: " . . . he was of that rare kind who look not for reward, but for opportunity, and he came to the call of the work."[37] Osborne added to his income by taking charge of St. Paul's Church, Monroe, preaching occasionally at Trinity Church, Statesville, and conducting services at St. Michael's and All Angels congregation in Charlotte. He was also the "local agent at Charlotte" for the Aetna Life Insurance Company.[38]

THE DREAM BECOMES OBSESSION

In his autobiography, Edwin Osborne revealed:

> Soon after I took charge of St. Mark's Church, a thought which had before occurred to me returned with more than usual disturbances. It was that the Church have an orphanage in North Carolina, and with the thought, to start the enterprise.[39]

During his years as Clerk of the Superior Court, from 1866 to 1875, Edwin Osborne had witnessed at first hand the state's provision for dependent and orphaned children as he administered the laws relating to apprenticeship, guardianship and the care of childrens' properties. According to the apprenticeship acts of 1715 and 1755, still observed past the end of the nineteenth century, an orphan whose estate was so small that no person would undertake to educate or maintain him was to be bound as an apprentice, "every male to some Tradesman, Merchant, Mariner, or other person approved by the Court, until he shall attain the Age of Twenty-one Years, and every Female to some Suitable Employment, til her Age of Eighteen Years . . . "[40] There was a wide range of trades to which children were apprenticed, although the most prevalent were "the art and mystery of farming" or "the art and mystery of housewifery."[41] With the establishment of factories, children were also employed as factory hands at rates as low as 12 ½ cents a week.[42]

Orphans' court was held once a year in each county, although after the Constitution of 1868, authority for administering the affairs of orphans and apprenticed children in Mecklenburg was consolidated under the Superior Court rather than a separate County Court.[43] Despite the new constitution's declaration that, "There shall . . . be measures devised by the State for the establishment of one or more Orphan Houses, where destitute orphans may be cared for, educated and taught some business or trade,"[44] no action was taken to carry out the mandate. Instead, the establishment of orphanages was a task quickly relegated to the private sector, most notably to religious organizations. Apparently recognizing that establishment of a state-supported orphanage was unlikely, Governor Tod R. Caldwell, in his message to the General Assembly of 1873-1874 affirmed the role of private agencies:

It is well known that very few bound orphans are ever sent to any school, and that most of them are growing up in ignorance of the laws of God and of the laws of their country. Having lost their natural guides and protectors, and feeling that society has failed to afford them the means of improvement, they naturally sink into vice and degration [sic] and become a plague and a burden to the State. But when destitute orphans learn their obligations to God and to their fellow-

men, and are taught to support themselves by some honorable occupation, they rise above those temptations which usually ensnare the ignorant, and become useful and respectable citizens. The Constitution therefore sanctions sound suitable provision for the protection and training of the multitude of fatherless, motherless, friendless and penniless orphans, whose sad and sorrowful silence should be their most eloquent advocate.[45]

Fired with the vision to provide an orphanage under the direction of the Episcopal church, Edwin Osborne sought practical ways to undertake the project. He recorded in his autobiography: "But I did not see how I could start such an undertaking as I had no money and [I was] not acquainted with any moneyed men who would likely be interested in such an enterprise."[46] Then he thought of his former pastor and friend, Benjamin S. Bronson, who still held in trust the old Thompson Institute property along Charlotte's Sugar Creek. Bronson wanted the land to be used for some church endeavor and had offered it to Joseph Cheshire in 1881:

Joseph Blount Cheshire

21

Shortly after coming to Charlotte, Mr. Bronson wrote me that I could have the property for any church work, if I would assume the indebtedness resting upon it. I felt too seriously the importance of my parochial and pastoral work to be willing to burden myself at that time with additional responsibilities, and I declined Mr. Bronson's offer.[47]

Bronson made a similar offer to Edwin Osborne in 1885, just after he had returned to Charlotte to take over St. Mark's mission. With the nagging dream in his head of establishing an orphanage and Benjamin Bronson's letter in his hand, Edwin Osborne went to Joseph Cheshire, who recalled:

He came to me with Mr. Bronson's letter, and proposed that we should accept Mr. Bronson's offer, and establish an orphanage to be maintained as a Diocesan institution. I replied that I had too much parochial and missionary work on hand to think of assuming additional responsibilities, but I assured him of my hearty sympathy with him and promised my cordial co-operation if he would assume the leadership and responsibility in the work.[48]

Osborne then asked Benjamin Bronson if he would be willing to convey the property to the diocese for an orphanage. "Yes," came the reply, on two conditions: one, that the name 'Thompson' be preserved; and two, that the Rev. Edwin Osborne be responsible for setting up the orphanage and serve as its superintendent.[49]

THE DIOCESE OF NORTH CAROLINA UNDERTAKES AN ORPHANAGE

With the endorsement of Bishop Theodore Lyman, the orphanage proposal was taken up at the Seventieth Annual Convention of the Diocese of North Carolina, held May 19-23, 1886 at Calvary Church, Tarboro. A special committee was appointed May 19 to study a resolution which would convey to the trustees of the diocese deeds to property in Charlotte held by Benjamin Bronson and by the vestry of St. Peter's Church for establishing "an Orphanage and Industrial Institution."[50] Members of that committee included Bishop Theodore Lyman, Edwin Osborne, Joseph Cheshire, and attorneys R.H. Battle, Col. W.H.S. Burgwyn, and Bronson's legal advisor Hugh Murray.

On May 21 the Convention, on the unanimous report of the committee, approved the resolution. The trustees paid $1 for the approximately 61 acres held by Benjamin and Alice Bronson, and agreed to relieve St. Peter's Church of its mortgage debt of $1,000, originally borrowed by the rector.[51]

According to the Canons, trustees of the diocese were "the Bishop, or when there is no Bishop, the President of the Standing Committee . . . ex-officio, with two laymen to be elected by the Convention".[52] The trustees were "authorized to hold the property of the Diocese not otherwise provided for."[53] The trustees of the Diocese of North Carolina who accepted, in 1886, the deeds to the property for the Thompson Orphanage were the Rt. Rev. Theodore B. Lyman, R.H. Battle, and W.E. Anderson.

The business of operating the diocese's orphanage was entrusted to a Board of Managers, the first members of which were appointed at the Convention: the Rt. Rev. Theodore B. Lyman, ex-officio; the Rev. W.R. Wetmore, Lincolnton, for 6 years; the Rev. Joseph B. Cheshire, Jr., Charlotte, for 2 years; the Rev. Edwin A. Osborne, Charlotte, for 4 years; F.M. Garrett, King's Mountain, for 6 years; Baxter H. Moore, Charlotte, for 4 years; and James F. Payne, Monroe, for 2 years.[54]

ORPHANAGE MOVEMENT GROWS

The orphanage and training institution established by the Episcopal Diocese of North Carolina in 1886 was among the forerunners in a phenomenon of orphanage development which embraced a fifty year period between 1875 and 1925, being the fourth such institution in the state. While there are occasional references during the early part of the nineteenth century to other orphanages or orphan asylum societies in the state, these were of short duration. The state's first permanent institution, the Oxford Orphan Asylum, was opened in February, 1873, by the Grand Lodge of the Order of Free Masons. In 1883 the Grant Colored Asylum, later incorporated as The Colored Orphanage Asylum of North Carolina, opened near Oxford, a project of the American Baptist Publication Society of Philadelphia, the Wake Baptist Association, and the Shiloh Baptist Association of

North Carolina. The Mills Home at Thomasville, later known as the Baptist Orphanage, accepted its first child on November 11, 1885.[55]

On Friday, July 9, 1886 the front page of the *Charlotte Evening Chronicle* announced:

> A movement is on foot to establish at this place a home for orphan and destitute children within our borders. Just outside of the city limits, on Trade street, is a piece of property containing about seventy two acres, and is known as the Bronson place . . . The necessary buildings are already upon the property and it is considered an admirable place for the purpose . . . While the management will be under members of the Episcopal church of this State yet its not proposed to make it an orphanage for that denomination alone. It will be open to all and be designed to aid the poor and destitute as far as possible . . . With an Orphan Asylum and [sic] Oxford and an Orphanage at Thomasville, and the one proposed here, it would seem that this class of children in North Carolina will be well provided for by our people.[56]

On August 10, 1886, the Board of Managers for the Thompson Orphanage and Training Institution held its first meeting in Charlotte. In his 1887 address to the diocesan Convention, Bishop Theodore Lyman reported:

> We spent some time in discussing the most feasible plans, and had a very satisfactory meeting. The Institution will speedily be opened, and I confidently believe that it will awaken, throughout the Diocese, that interest and sympathy, — that thoughtful care, which it so greatly needs, and to which it is so justly entitled.[57]

According to the minutes of that first meeting, Bishop Theodore Lyman directed Edwin Osborne and Joseph Cheshire to prepare a constitution and by-laws to govern the institution. A committee of three men from each parish of the diocese was proposed to represent the interests of the orphanage in the various communities and elicit financial support. Capt. Baxter H. Moore and James F. Payne were appointed to serve with Edwin Osborne and Joseph Cheshire as an Executive Committee, and Capt. Moore was elected Secretary-Treasurer.

In the final business of the day, the Board members officially affirmed Edwin Osborne as superintendent of the orphanage and set his salary at $300 a year.

As the Board meeting ended, Edwin Osborne rose and stretched, welcoming the slight, dust-filled breeze that met him outside.

He watched the wagons plodding east along Trade Street toward the intersection with Tryon where on such warm afternoons, Charlotte's gentlemen kept court outdoors, their chairs tilted carelessly against the stonework.[58] A few blocks further, just outside the city limits along Sugar Creek and below the Myers Plantation, the wagons would pass the old Bronson place where soon the forbidding tangle of weeds and underbrush would be flattened under the feet of laughing children.

A smile broke the corners of his mouth as he started home toward Graham Street, measuring with each step the remarkable evolution of a singular dream.

FOOTNOTES

1. Mary Norton Kratt, *Charlotte: Spirit of the New South* (Tulsa: Continental Heritage Press, 1980), p. 161.

2. Hugh Talmage Lefler and Albert Ray Newsome, *The History of a Southern State — North Carolina,* 3rd ed. (Chapel Hill, University of North Carolina Press, 1973), p. 319

3. Ibid.

4. Lefler and Newsome, p. 416.

5. Bertie County Court, "Tribute to Lewis Thompson," February, 1868.

6. Lefler and Newsome, p. 323.

7. Joseph Carlyle Sitterson, "Lewis Thompson, A Carolinian and His Louisiana Plantation, 1848-1888: A Study In Absentee Ownership," in James Sprunt, *Studies In History and Political Science,* ed. Fletcher Melvingreen, Vol. 31 (Chapel Hill: University of North Carolina Press, 1949), p. 18.

8. Mary Bond Griffin, "Reminiscence," prepared for the Thompson Orphanage Jubilee Celebration, May 7, 1937.

9. Mary Bond Thompson to Lewis Thompson, July 25, 1860, Lewis Thompson Papers in the Southern Historical Collection, University of North Carolina Library, Chapel Hill, N.C.

10. Joseph Blount Cheshire, copy of an unidentified newspaper clipping, circa April 21, 1918, attached to minutes of the Executive Committee, April 21, 1918.

11. Ibid.

12. Joseph Blount Cheshire, *St. Peter's Church, Charlotte, N.C., Historical Addresses From Colonial Days to 1893* (Charlotte: Observer Printing House, 1921), p. 24.

13. D. A. Thompkins, *History of Mecklenburg County and the City of Charlotte From 1740-1903* (Charlotte: Observer Printing House, 1903), p. 151.

14. Joseph Blount Cheshire, *The Church in the Confederate States* (New York: Longmans, Green, & Co., 1912), pp. 93, 100-102.

15. Ibid.

16. Lefler and Newsome, p. 477.

17. Benjamin S. Bronson to Lewis Thompson, circa April 23, 1867, Lewis Thompson Papers, Southern Historical Collection, University of North Carolina Library, Chapel Hill, N.C.

18. Alan D. Watson, *Bertie County — A Brief History* (Raleigh: Division of Archives and History, North Carolina Department of Cultural Affairs, 1982), p. 82.

19. Deed Book 5, p. 233, Mecklenburg County Register of Deeds Office, Charlotte, N.C.

20. Thompkins, p. 166.

21. "Raleigh Correspondence of the Democrat," *The Western Democrat,* December 17, 1867, p. 2.

22. Bertie County Court, "Tribute," February, 1868.

23. The gift is assumed to have been at least $2,000. The first purchase of additional land Bronson made following receipt of this gift was for 57 acres from W.B. and Hassie Thomas at a cost of $2,000.

24. Cheshire, *Historical Addresses,* p. 25.

25. Deed Book 6, page 76 and Deed Book 47, p. 598, Mecklenburg County Register of Deeds Office, Charlotte, N.C.

26. Cheshire, *Historical Addresses,* p. 25.

27. "The History of The Thompson Orphanage, and Training Institution," *The Carolina Churchman,* October, 1911, p. 6.

28. Rev. Norvin C. Duncan, *Pictorial History Of The Episcopal Church In North Carolina, 1701-1964* (Asheville: Miller Printing Co., 1965), p. 85.

29. Dr. William H. Huffman, "A Historical Sketch of the Good Samaritan Hospital", April, 1983, Thompson Orphanage Historical Files.

30. "The Charlotte Orphanage," *Charlotte Evening Chronicle,* July 9, 1886, p. 1.

31. Edwin Augustus Osborne, unpublished autobiography from the private papers of Francis O. Clarkson, Charlotte, N.C. (Hereinafter cited as "Autobiography.")

32. Lawrence Foushee London, *Bishop Joseph Blount Cheshire, His Life and Work* (Chapel Hill: University of North Carolina Press, 1941), p. 27.

33. Joseph Blount Cheshire, *St. Mark's Church, Mecklenburg County, North Carolina — Its Beginnings: 1884-1886,* (n.p.) p. 6.

34. Edwin Osborne, "Autobiography," p. 113.

35. Cheshire, *Historical Addresses,* p. 36.

36. Edwin Osborne, "Autobiography," p. 114.

37. Cheshire, *Historical Addresses,* p. 36.

38. Advertisement, *The Western Democrat,* February, 18, 1868, p. 1.

39. Edwin Osborne, "Autobiography," p. 116.

40. Arthur E. Fink, "Changing Philosophies and Practices in North Carolina Orphanages," in *North Carolina Historical Review,* XLVIII, No. 4 (Raleigh: Division of Archives and History, North Carolina Department of Cultural Affairs, October, 1971), 334.

41. Ibid., p. 335

42. Guion Griffis Johnson, *Ante-Bellum North Carolina* (Chapel Hill: University of North Carolina Press, 1937), p. 255.

43. Edwin Osborne, "Autobiography," p. 110.

44. Fink, p. 336.

45. Ibid., p. 337.

46. Edwin Osborne, "Autobiography," p. 116.

47. Cheshire, *Historical Addresses,* pp. 28-29.

48. Ibid., p. 39.

49. Edwin Osborne, "Autobiography," p. 116.

50. *Journal of the Seventieth Annual Convention of the Protestant Episcopal Church in the Diocese of North Carolina, May 19-22, 1886,* (Raleigh: Edwards, Broughton & Co, Printers, 1886), p. 47. (Hereinafter cited as Journal.)

51. Ibid., pp. 25, 47-48.

52. *Journal,* 1886, p. 107.

53. Ibid.

54. Ibid., p. 6.

55. Fink, pp. 337-339.

56. "The Charlotte Orphanage," p. 1.

57. "Bishop's Address," *Journal,* 1887, p. 9.

58. Dannye Romine, *Mecklenburg: A Bicentennial Story* (Charlotte: Independence Square Associates, 1975), p. 57.

Chapter 2

"No Longer An Experiment"

1886 — 1898

Sunlight fell harshly across the page, rebounding from the covering of snow which lay across the campus. Inside the painfully chill room, Edwin Osborne put down the pen and cupped his hands to his mouth, warming them with his breath. He knew it was just the cold that made the writing difficult, having long ago learned to compensate for the missing fingers on his right hand, a remembrance by their absence of Spotsylvania Court House.[1]

Outside, the early spring snow which had fallen undisturbed along Sugar Creek suddenly became a wintry playground of ice forts and snow angels as the children came out to play, attacking the white powder with an eagerness usually reserved only for mealtime.

He sighed heavily, realizing he had been thinking in metaphors of war for he, too, had been infected by the familiar, blustering jingoism of 1898.

Putting away the day's accounts, Osborne reached for his Superintendent's Record Book, the journal he'd kept since the opening of the Thompson Orphanage 12 years ago. His hand moved across its worn cover, his fingers studying

the swirls of colorful half-moons in unending, uneven rows. He had planned to spend the afternoon making new entries but as he turned the pages, the memories spilled out.

During his first months as superintendent of the Thompson Orphanage and Training Institution in 1886, Edwin Osborne had, by his own admission, "nothing to superintend."[2]

> There was only a tract of land, a brick yard rented to a Negro man whose name was Houser, two or three brick cabins in very bad condition occupied by Negroes, a large brick residence and a good school building, all in bad state of repair, no furniture and not a dollar to begin with.[3]

Conditions at the Thompson Orphanage site were made only slightly worse by an earthquake which rumbled through Charlotte on August 31, 1886, further damaging the old Thompson Hall.

The initial challenge facing the new orphanage superintendent was to raise funds for necessary repairs and furnishings. At the December 30, 1886 meeting of the Board of Managers, Edwin Osborne was authorized, "to use such means as may be necessary to raise funds for the support of the Orphanage, and bring it to the attention of the public."[4] The Board allowed for travel and other expenses to come from the treasury. On the strength of his reputation as a respected citizen, churchman, and former Confederate Army officer, Edwin Osborne went from house to house throughout Charlotte asking for contributions and pledges of support for the orphanage. Many who could not give money made donations of clothing, furniture and other equipment. He then took his campaign to other cities across the state including Raleigh, Henderson, Weldon and Wilmington. Since he traveled at his own expense, the free pass extended by Major John C. Winder, vice president and general manager of the Seaboard Railway, was a valuable contribution.[5]

In his report to the Convention of the Diocese of North Carolina in May, 1887, Edwin Osborne documented his success:

> In response to these efforts I have received many assurances of the sympathy and approval of our people, as well as much material aid. A great many Parishes in North Carolina and a few in East Carolina, have sent contributions in money, and many North Carolina Parishes have sent boxes of valuable supplies for the institution.[6]

SUPPORT GROWS

Individuals who made significant gifts during this time included Col. Hamilton C. Jones, junior warden of St. Peter's Church, Mrs. Ann Lardner, and former state supreme court judge William Preston Bynum of Charlotte, David Y. Cooper of Henderson, Lawrence Holt of Burlington, and the children of Lewis Thompson — Thomas, William, and Mary Bond Thompson Urquhart of Bertie County.[8] One of the first donations, recorded in the Superintendent's Record was for $5 from the Rev. W.S. Bynum, given as a memorial to "dear little Katie" on September 14, 1886. A note later squeezed into the margin by Edwin Osborne indicated how the money was spent: "Bought a wagon with this for Mary Capps, a cripple in the Orphanage."[9] Every gift was duly and graciously noted: "one bedstead," "four benches for chapel," "use of carriage," "1 bed quilt," "bushel of potatoes," "sup-ply slates and pencils," "sack of flour," "knit stockings," "ton of coal." Free medical care was supplied by Dr. Simmons B. Jones.

During 1886, Osborne collected enough funds and pledges to repair Thompson Hall and add to it a two-story front porch, a kitchen and another bedroom. To the 1887 Diocesan Convention he reported:

> I have received the sum of $747.58 and expended in traveling expenses, material and repairs on the house, $183.58, leaving a balance on hand of $563.76. I have been compelled to add a great many additional repairs, which will, with the necessary articles for furnishing the house, amount to four or five hundred dollars more.[10]

His travels across the state raised more than money for Thompson Orphanage; they brought awareness and commitments of continued support, particularly from the women of Episcopal congregations who formed themselves into guilds to help sustain the institution. Among the first were St. Peter's Church Guild in Charlotte and the St. Agnes Guild of Christ Church, Raleigh. Chief organizers were Mrs. Mary Mason Bryan of Raleigh, Miss Emma J. Hall and Miss Augusta Boyd of Charlotte, and Miss Rebecca "Aunt Becky" Cameron of Hillsborough.[11]

While on a visit to Durham, Osborne also found the orphanage's first matron, Miss Elizabeth J. Mackay. "After a few minutes' conversation," he decided she was most suitable for the position, and hired her for $15 a month.[12] As he recalled:

> Miss Mackay and I had been brought up in the country and had gone through the trials and privations of the Confederate War, and she had come out brave, strong and self-reliant, and proved to be the very woman for the place and the time.[13]

Miss Mackay, "as her firm mouth testifies, she was the real boss of the works," remembered Edwin Osborne's daughter Josephine.[14]

"LET THE LITTLE CHILDREN COME TO ME"

The official opening date for the Thompson Orphanage and Training Institution was May 7, 1887, chosen as nearest Edwin Osborne's May 6 birthday. The first children received at the orphanage, on May 9, 1887, were Lawrence Caldwell of Charlotte, age 7 and Jennie Jones from Cleveland County, age 2. During the next two days the Davis children of Charlotte were admitted: Ida, 10, Walter, 8, and Mary, 7,

Elizabeth J. Mackay, first matron

followed on May 25 and June 3 by brothers William Jonathan and Benjamin Hall Brewer, ages 7 and 4, who were brought from the Mecklenburg County Poorhouse.

Sometime prior to its formal opening, the Thompson Orphanage had served as a refuge for the Helms family children, traditionally regarded as the institution's first residents. Though there is no record of them in the *Superintendent's Record,* Edwin Osborne's daughter Josephine remembered the incident.

> Of course I was very small in 1886 when the place was begun, but I well recall the first inmates — name of Helms — poor street waifs with only an ignorant old man dragging them about. They spent the first night at our home where were placed palates on the parlor floor, and we gave them breakfast before they trailed out across the town and spent all their childhood . . . at the orphanage.[15]

Accounts differ as to whether there were three or five children in the family.

Josephine Osborne

It is not insignificant that the Thompson Orphanage shared its founding year with the dedication of the Statue of Liberty in New York's harbor. As the 'Lady with the Lamp' stood as a symbol to the world's tired, poor, "huddled masses yearning to breathe free," the Thompson Orphanage was, in miniature, a working example for North Carolina's homeless, deserted, and destitute children.

From the very first, applicants for admission to the orphanage far exceeded its capacity. With six children already in residence, the superintendent reported to the Diocese, "I have the names of a considerable number of others who are in need of a home. We can only accommodate about twenty-five or thirty in our present buildings . . . "[16] Those who were admitted came from every section of the state, "from poorhouses, from poverty-stricken homes, from neglect . . . rescued in some instances from dens of infamy and vice."[17] Many were truly orphans, while others had at least one living parent.

As soon as the institution was opened, there were numerous "applications for children" recorded by the superintendent. Most were from people requesting an older child who could work as a farm hand, household maid, or companion, although some wanted a child to adopt.

> R.E. ———, Charlotte, wants a boy to adopt as his own.
> Mrs. Fox wants a well trained girl.
> Miss A.L. ———, Lincolnton wants a little girl ten years old for her mother.
> Mrs. A.B. ——— and a friend each want a child. Mrs. F. wants a little girl or boy about six years old, and her friend wants one about twelve.
> Mr. B.W. ——— of Huntersville, N.C. wants a boy bound to him on farm.
> Mrs. Jerome ——— wants girl 10 or 12 years old, as nurse and help.
> Mrs. Dave ———, Concord, N.C. wants an orphan under five years old to adopt.[18]

A few children were "placed out" with individuals who promised to supply "food, clothing and education," but very often the childrens' records read, "returned to the orphanage." For the majority, Thompson Orphanage was simply, home. They lived at the institution until they received sufficient education and training to earn a living, or until discharged to parents or relatives who could again support them.

These first children, regularly referred to as "inmates", found caring though spartan living conditions, as described by Edwin Osborne:

> . . . a lot of old cast-off furniture and bedding, and a lot of old second hand clothing of all sizes, fashions, colors and conditions, no running water, kerosene lamps and candles for light, a small second hand cooking stove and very plain, cheap tableware and oilcloth covers."[19]

Considered crucial needs at the time were a

residence for the superintendent and additional buildings for the children, farm stock and implements, and the payment of about $500 in debts on the property. The Diocesan Convention in 1887 set up a mechanism to help ensure annual financial support by authorizing that the Thanksgiving offerings in each parish and mission be devoted to the Thompson Orphanage, and that clergy "call the attention of their congregations to the importance of this Christ-like charity and their responsibility in sustaining it liberally."[20]

UP FROM "DEGRADATION AND RUIN"

Untiring in his efforts and enthusiasm for the orphanage, Edwin Osborne inspired others with visions of its success.

> The promise of usefulness for this work is good, and the necessity for it is urgent. Wherever I have been I have heard of little homeless children growing up in neglect and destitution, whose end must, unless they are cared for, generally be degradation and ruin; but who, in such an institution as this is designed to be, might in a few years become useful members of the Church and of society.[21]

After its first full year in operation, the Thompson Orphanage had 30 children in residence and, noted the superintendent, "the building is full."[22] The cost of care for each child was estimated by Edwin Osborne at $60 a year, or $1,800, on the supposition that the children would be supplied with all necessary clothing by the women of the Diocese.

> The women of the Diocese, as might have been expected, have done a noble part by this institution. In addition to their liberal contributions in money, they have been untiring in their labors, collecting subscriptions and procuring supplies in the way of clothing, bedding, etc ... I estimate that the supplies in kind that have come from all these sources, in addition to the money, will amount to at least one thousand dollars in value.[23]

During 1888, Edwin Osborne raised about $1,600, enough to build a new wood frame cottage for the younger children, completed in January 1890, which he named Bronson Hall. He also added "a comfortable eight-room, two-story residence for the Superintendent and also a very good two-story barn."[24] A wire fence was put up around the main building and a large piece of the bottom land used as a cow pasture. Other improvements included a brick dairy and a brick washroom which, according to Osborne's daughter Josephine, "must have been luxuries untold, especially as before that they had to attend to such tasks out-doors."[25]

An increased staff was quickly necessary to accommodate the growing institution. During 1888, a Miss Fleming was hired as a teacher for the older children, conducting classes for a portion of each school day when the children were not working. Her salary was $100 for the ten months of schooling provided. An assistant matron was added at $84 a year, and Andrew Rodden came on as foreman of the orphanage farm, receiving an annual salary of $200. Other additions included one mule and two cows.

PARISH AND ORPHANAGE RESPONSIBILITIES

Throughout this early period in the orphanage's development, Edwin Osborne maintained his parochial duties in addition to serving as superintendent. In 1887 he was missionary for St. Mark's Mission in Mecklenburg County, St. John's Church in Rutherfordton, and Church of the Redeemer in Shelby, and continued to preach at Trinity Church, Statesville and serve the congregation at St. Paul's Church in Monroe. In that same year, he held about 40 services at the orphanage and baptized 13 children. As he traveled about the state canvassing for the Thompson Orphanage he also assisted in the services and preached at the local churches.

In May, 1888, Osborne appealed to the Diocesean Convention:

> The work of the Orphanage has now become so immense as to require all the time and attention of one person to attend to its duties properly, and I am compelled to ask that I may be relieved of some of my missionary work, or else that some one be appointed in my place as Superintendent of the Orphanage. I would very much prefer the latter suggestion, as the work of the Orphanage interferes very much with my ministerial duties and obligations.[26]

Thompson Hall, made with Sugar Creek bricks

As chairman of the Board of Managers, Bishop Joseph Cheshire, in a meeting on November 20, 1888, acceded to part of the superintendent's request, asking that he give up his pastoral work outside the bounds of Mecklenburg County. Osborne's salary was also to be raised to $600 a year to help compensate for giving up some of his ministerial responsibilities. His offer of resignation was declined by the Board.

The committee which received and commented on his second annual report to the Diocesan Convention continued to express satisfaction with the choice of Edwin Osborne as superintendent.

> To its most faithful and untiring Superintendent cannot be accorded too much credit in pushing to the foremost place in the Diocese its noblest institution of charity, and in opening before it such a cheering prospect of a still larger field of usefulness in the near future.[27]

By 1889 there were 39 children living in Thompson Hall and, although physical conditions were cramped, a visitor to the campus observed, "the bright faces of happy children greet you at every turn. Some are busy helping the farmer, some engaged in the laundry, and some in the kitchen. Others are found in the school room, others still on the playground. All are contented and happy."[28]

ENTERING THE NINETIES

As the institution prepared to enter the last decade of the nineteenth century known as 'the Gay Nineties,' life for the orphanage children was, if not gay, at least more promising. The superintendent observed in 1890:

> The children are growing rapidly, and developing in mind and character, and I rejoice to add, also in moral and spiritual growth. Ten were confirmed at the last visitation and we now have twelve communicants among the children.[29]

Although affiliation with the Episcopal church was not an entrance requirement, great emphasis was placed on baptism and confirmation. The first eleven children in the orphanage were quickly baptized in the small chapel in Thompson Hall on August 31, 1887, Elizabeth J. Mackay serving as each child's sponsor.

The orphanage took on total responsibility for each child's physical, social, religious, and recreational needs as well as for education and training. With the state's economy pressed continually toward industrialization since the close of the Civil War, Osborne recognized the need to provide the children with adequate training. The farm offered "pleasant and healthful employment for the boys" while the girls practiced domestic arts such as cooking, washing and sewing. "But," explained Osborne to the Diocesan convention in 1891, "we feel the need of some other kinds of industry, in order to fit them for a higher sphere of usefulness and happiness than can usually be procured by domestic labor in this section of our country."[30] He proposed establishing a "steam laundry, knitting factory, or other industry" on campus, to train the girls for the rapidly changing focus of the state's economy, as well as to "contribute in some measure to the support of the Orphanage."[31]

Some of the children even aspired to, and where possible, received, higher education.

> One of our girls is at Claremont College, Hickory, where she has been for two terms, through the assistance of the Guilds in Charlotte and Hickory, and the generosity of the proprietor of the school. She desires to become a teacher, and Mr. Sanborn, after keeping her two terms at about half rates, is now keeping her for the present term without charge, rather than to disappoint her aims.[32]

Edwin Osborne continued to enlist that additional buildings and services were necessary for effective operation of the institution, including an industrial hall for boys, a chapel, a playroom for the children in bad weather, and an infirmary.

> One thing we need most urgently is an infirmary. We have no suitable place for our sick, and in case of contagion the whole school is at the mercy of the disease.[33]

He also desired printing equipment and supplies "in order that we may publish a paper and train some of the children in the art of printing.'[34]

Since the opening of the orphanage, its superintendent had appealed to the Diocese of North Carolina for an endowment fund to help support the needs of the institution. He was particularly embarrassed at soliciting funds which would be used to cover his own salary.[35] A special committee of the Convention, which had for some time been considering the matter of establishing such a fund, reported in 1890 "that in their opinion it is not expedient to take such action at present."[36]

The Diocesan Convention of 1890 did, however, affirm a resolution to more clearly involve the Diocese of East Carolina in the operation and support of the Thompson Orphanage and Training Institution. The resolution came from a March 22, 1890 recommendation by the or-

Original Bronson Hall

phanage Board of Managers that the Bishop of East Carolina be appointed an ex-officio member of the Board of Managers, and that East Carolina nominate one clerical and one lay member "to cooperate in making the Thompson Orphanage a joint institution of the two Dioceses . . . "[37] The reasons for the proposal were outlined at the Convention:

> First, the donor of the money with which the land was purchased on which the Orphanage stands, was a resident of that part of the State which now forms the Diocese of East Carolina. Secondly, the deed conveying the property to this Diocese for the purposes of an Orphanage, provides that the Institution shall be for the benefit of homeless children in the State of North Carolina. Thirdly, the taking part in the management of the Orphanage by the Diocese of East Carolina would not only promote that cordial good feeling between the two Dioceses, which all desire, but it would also be a real bond of union, in the formation of which surely all hearts will rejoice, between brethren once forming a single family, but now separated into two.[38]

ST. MARY'S CHAPEL

Throughout his first three years at Thompson Orphanage, Edwin Osborne appealed to the Diocesan Conventions for a new chapel. In 1889 he wrote, "At present we hold services in the school room, but it is difficult to impress children with proper ideas of reverence and devotion under such circumstances."[39] Not long afterward his friend, Judge William Preston Bynum, who had served as solicitor of the Ninth Judicial District at the time Osborne was Clerk of Superior Court, gave the orphanage what Osborne considered "one of the noblest and most valuable contributions"; $2,500 for a chapel.[40] The money was given as a memorial to his late wife Eliza and daughter Mary Shipp Bynum.

Osborne "procured the plan and selected the location, [for the new chapel] choosing the site on account of its accessibility to the public and remoteness from other buildings."[41] The chapel was constructed between April, 1891 and the summer of 1892, built with bricks apparently made from clay dug at the orphanage and fired there, evidenced by distinctive black marks made during the drying process and the fact that

there were "an inordinate number" of bricks used in the extremely thick foundation and walls.[42]

Even before it was finished, the chapel courtyard became a final resting place for two orphanage residents. The first was five-year old Willie Love of Wilmington, a child with no living parents who arrived at Thompson Orphanage in February, 1891. Records show she died January 9, 1890 of severe burns received when she fell into the open grate of a fireplace. Six months later, Bronson Hall matron Irene Cecelia Mackay died of consumption at the age of 24. Another child, eight-year old Hugh Whitfield Beaver of Salisbury, died from measles on January 15, 1896 and was also buried in the church yard next to Willie Love. These graves were eventually moved to Elmwood Cemetery in 1900, though they weren't marked with headstones until 1922.

With a chapel under construction, Bronson Hall filled to capacity, and church contributions mounting, however slowly, Edwin Osborne was able to affirm with confidence in 1892, "The Orphanage is no longer an experiment. It has become a permanent and prominent feature of the work of the church of the State of North Carolina."[43]

The Board of Managers agreed with the assessment, observing that the superintendent and his staff "have set the life of the little orphans to music, judging from their orderly ways and happy faces."[44]

EXCITEMENT AND EXPANSION

Osborne expressed a renewed exuberance over the operation of the institution in his 1894 annual report. There were 66 children in the orphanage during 1893-94, more than in any previous year. Contributions, both in money and material donations, were also greater than ever before. Although the cotton crop was a near failure, the orphanage made up for the loss in sales of farm produce including vegetables, milk and butter.. "We now have a dairy in successful operation," he reported, "which furnishes an abundance of milk for the children and some for the market; splendid training for the boys and fine manures for the land." The year was marred only by the loss of a mule, struck by lightning in June, 1893.

Although dependent on donations for its existence, the Thompson Orphanage contributed to its own support as much as possible, raising and selling cotton, turnips, dairy products and other farm produce, selling sand and gravel to local contractors, renting land to William H. Houser for his brickyard, and publishing the *Messenger of Hope* diocesan newspaper which, by 1895, boasted 2,000 subscribers.

The children of Thompson Orphanage were a familiar sight driving their donkey cart, filled with farm produce, through Charlotte's streets. " . . . They went out day after day," remembered Josephine Osborne, "and father invented all sorts of things for them to sell — turnip seed in quantity, for instance!"[45]

Fifteen children were discharged from the orphanage during 1893, four of whom were reported to have "good positions . . . earning from 75 cents to one dollar a day" Others were placed in good homes "with fair prospects of usefulness."[46]

To help protect the childrens' environment, the superintendent purchased a small strip of land in April, 1893 which lay between the boundary of the orphanage property and the new Providence Road. The deed for the additional 1 ½ acres was given to the trustees of the Diocese of North Carolina to be included in the total of orphanage property.[47]

Maintaining the buildings on campus was a constant necessity, and as the orphanage population grew, there were more and more demands for repairs, increased space and new facilities. The school, for example, was held in the same classroom originally used by Benjamin Bronson between 1868 and 1873. Here the children faced a challenge nearly as great as their academic studies: trying to keep their pencils from rolling away and becoming hopelessly lost in the deep cracks of the old wooden floor.[48]

Miss Kate Capehart, one of the institution's most popular matrons, began work at Thompson Orphanage as a teacher in 1893-1894, later taking over for Mrs. Sargent as matron for Bronson Hall. During the next school term Miss Estelle "Essie" Call, a girl who had received most of her education at the Thompson Or-

The donkey cart was a familiar sight along Charlotte streets

phanage, being admitted in 1888 at age 11, joined the staff.

A donation of $2,500 from the Bishop Atkinson Memorial Cot Fund in December, 1893, was quickly set aside for building improvements, including a greatly-expanded school classroom. The money was collected as a memorial to Bishop Atkinson by Sarah Rebecca "Aunt Becky" Cameron from Sunday School children across the state she called her 'Messengers of Hope.' Originally intended for St. John's Hospital in Raleigh, the fund was donated to the Thompson Orphanage when the hospital was bought by the city of Raleigh.

A two-story addition to Thompson Hall was constructed in 1894 using money from the Bishop Atkinson Fund. It included a large dining hall, pantry, storeroom, kitchen, ironing room and dormitory for girls on the south side, and a boys' dormitory and a room for the matrons on the west end. The old dining room was converted to a "large and comfortable hall for a study and work-room,"[49] and the old classroom was expanded, taking over space formerly used as the boys' dormitory. A new slate roof was put on the old sections of the building to match the new additions.

At about the same time, the orphanage chapel was officially dedicated, having been in use since the end of 1892. It was consecrated May 1, 1895, feast day of St. Philip and St. James, by the Rt. Rev. Joseph B. Cheshire, Bishop of the Diocese of North Carolina, as 'The Memorial Chapel of St. Mary the Virgin.' Superintendent

Osborne reported to the diocese, "A large congregation witnessed the impressive ceremonies of consecration and the confirmation of six girls and five boys, inmates of the institution." On the altar was a "beautiful wooden cross" donated in 1894 by Silas McBee, commissioner of the University of the South at Sewanee, another missionary institution of the Diocese of North Carolina.[50]

More building improvements were made possible by combining a legacy from Bishop Theodore Lyman, who died in 1893, and donations from the Thompson Orphanage Guild of St. Peter's Church in 1897. Among them was the addition of an infirmary to Thompson Hall in 1897, just in time to help isolate a siege of scarlet fever.

At their 1897 meeting on the orphanage campus, members of the Board of Managers were invited to visit with the children during lunch, enabling them to see at first hand the fruits of their work in behalf of the institution.

> The appearance and conduct of the children, as the members of the Board met them on the grounds and in buildings and conversed with them, bear ample testimony to the efficiency and faithfulness of those who have them in charge. Better-behaved children are not to be found anywhere.[51]

There remained one goal which, after 10 years, was still not realized. That was to make the orphanage into a 'training institution' as envisioned at its founding. Though Edwin Osborne had continually appealed for an industrial hall for boys, lack of money, equipment and teachers prohibited the plan from being carried out. Each day was sufficiently filled with the essentials of providing adequate food and clothing for the children "and such education as time allowed." [52] Except for spiritual guidance, which remained a priority, the orphanage could find little time, and even less money, for additional programs.

"REMEMBER THE MAINE"

While the century was winding down, a call to arms was rising throughout the United States in reaction to the sinking of the U.S. battleship "Maine" in Cuba's Havana harbor. Cries of outrage reached from the influential presses of New York and Washington, to the protected halls of the Thompson Orphanage, having their most profound effect upon the superintendent. President William McKinley's declaration of war against Spain, approved by Congress on April 20, 1898 avowed that the people of Cuba "are, and of right ought to be, free and independent," demanding that the government of Spain immediately relinquish its authority over the island. To enforce the declaration, the President was

'Balancing act' in front of old Bronson Hall

empowered to "use the entire land and naval forces of the United States, and to call into the actual service of the United States, the militia of the several States . . . "[53]

When the President called for 125,000 volunteers, "the response of North Carolina was immediate."[54] And among those who desired to serve was former Confederate officer, Edwin A. Osborne, who felt more confident in war than in the continuing battle he had experienced over the past 12 years between lack of finances and the orphanage's overwhelming needs. He asked the Board of Managers for an indefinite leave of absence.

> I was sorry to give up my position as Superintendent of the Orphanage at this time, but I thought I had occupied the position long enough for the good of the Institution and for my own good, as I did not wish to discontinue my calling as a minister of the Church. I also thought that my experience as a soldier in the Confederate War would enable me to be of special use to the men of the Regiment in case they should be engaged in active service in the Spanish-American War.[55]

Osborne was able to combine his battlefield experience and his calling as a minister by securing from the Rt. Rev. Joseph Cheshire, Bishop of the Diocese of North Carolina, an appointment as chaplain for the Second Regiment of North Carolina Volunteers under the command of Episcopal church layman and former Confederate colonel, W.H.S. Burgwyn. Osborne joined the much-maligned regiment in May, 1898 and moved with them to St. Simon's Island, Georgia until the troops were ordered back to Raleigh to be mustered out without ever firing a shot, their chief battle being with typhoid fever. "During my connection with the Regiment," recorded Osborne, "I was constantly engaged in preaching, visiting the men, and looking after the sick. Many of the men were sick and several died, and I buried them, using the burial service of the Church."[56]

Osborne's daughter Josephine wondered at her father's decision:

> To my child-like imaginings, I could not see the sense in giving up what I thought was 'his position,' so I asked him why . . . He replied that he had drained himself dry for the orphanage, and felt that it was provided for

Edwin Osborne's record book

so poorly that he thought best to let someone else try for a while. That he intended to recoupe his physical and mental self by life on a horse in the open air for a time. This agreed with him mighty well, besides he had no expenses, messed with the officers, was provided with necessary clothing, and the whole of $75.00 a month to recoup his finances![57]

The Thompson Orphanage was left in the care of its new superintendent, the Rev. Walter J. Smith, in June, 1898. Improvements swept in quickly during that year, flourishing on the foundation laid by Edwin Osborne and his dream of establishing a church-related orphanage in North Carolina.

In his first annual report to the diocese, Walter Smith affirmed the respect held at the Thompson Orphanage for its first superintendent, "whose heart is still in the work, and always will be. The continued devotion of the children to him is beautiful, and I hope it will never grow less."[58]

Still, a new century beckoned, and the Thompson Orphanage and Training Institution, no longer an experiment, faced new challenges and new leadership.

FOOTNOTES

1. According to a note from Francis Clarkson, a portion of Osborne's right hand was shot off in that battle.

2. Edwin Osborne, "Autobiography," p. 117.

3. Ibid.

4. Edwin Osborne, *Superintendent's Record*, p. 25.

5. Edwin Osborne, "Autobiography," p. 119.

6. *Journal,* 1887, p. 35.

7. Edwin Osborne, "Autobiography," p. 117.

8. Edwin Osborne, *Superintendent's Record*, p. 100.

9. Ibid., p. 160.

10. *Journal,* 1887, p. 35.

11. Edwin Osborne, "Autobiography," p. 118.

12. Ibid.

13. Ibid.

14. Josephine Osborne to Dr. Milton Barber, February 5, 1937, Thompson Orphanage Historical Files, Charlotte, N.C.

15. Ibid.

16. *Journal,* 1887, p. 35.

17. *Sketches of Church History in North Carolina — Addresses and Papers by Clergymen and Laymen of the Dioceses of North and East Carolina* (Wilmington, N.C.: William I. DeRosset, Jr., 1892), p. 330.

18. Edwin Osborne, *Superintendent's Record*, pp. 9-11.

19. Edwin Osborne, "Autobiography," p. 118.

20. *Journal,* 1887, p. 61.

21. Ibid., p. 35.

22. *Journal,* 1888, p. 44.

23. Ibid., pp. 45-46.

24. *Journal,* 1889, p. 31.

25. Josephine Osborne to Dr. Milton Barber, February 5, 1937.

26. *Journal,* 1888, p. 109.

27. *Journal,* 1889, p. 49.

28. *Sketches of Church History,* p. 329.

29. *Journal,* 1890, p. 30.

30. *Journal,* 1891, p. 44.

31. Ibid.

32. Ibid., p. 45.

33. *Journal,* 1889, p. 32.

34. Ibid., p. 33.

35. *Journal,* 1888, p. 44.

36. *Journal,* 1890, p. 66.

37. "Minutes," Board of Managers, Thompson Orphanage and Training Institution, March 22, 1890.

38. *Journal,* 1890, p. 29.

39. *Journal,* 1889, p. 33.

40. Edwin Osborne, "Autobiography," p. 119.

41. Ibid.

42. "Nomination of 'St. Mary The Virgin Memorial Chapel' As An Historic Site in Charlotte Mecklenburg," prepared by the Charlotte Mecklenburg Historic Properties Commission, circa 1974, Thompson Orphanage Historical Files, Charlotte, N.C.

43. *Journal,* 1892, p. 334.

44. *Journal,* 1893, p. 27.

45. Josephine Osborne to Dr. Milton Barber, February 5, 1937.

46. *Journal,* 1894, p. 44.

47. Deed Book 91, p. 343, Mecklenburg County Register of Deeds Office, Charlotte, N.C.

48. Josephine Osborne to Dr. Milton Barber, February 5, 1937.

49. *The Messenger of Hope,* September, 1894, p. 11.

50. *Eighth Annual Report of The Rev. E.A. Osborne, Superintendent of The Thompson Orphanage and Training Institution* (Charlotte: R.B. Elam Book and Job Printer, 1894), p. 15.

51. *Journal,* 1898, p. 27.

52. Josephine Osborne to Dr. Milton Barber, February 5, 1937.

53. "Recognition Of The Independence Of Cuba," *American Historical Documents,* The Harvard Classics, Charles W. Eliot, ed. (New York: P.F. Collier & Son Corp., 1938), pp. 440-441.

54. Joseph F. Stellman, *North Carolina's Role in the Spanish-American War* (Raleigh: Division of Archives and History, North Carolina Department of Cultural Affairs, 1975), p. 1.

55. Edwin Osborne, "Autobiography," p. 120.

56. Ibid.

57. Josephine Osborne to Dr. Milton Barber, February 5, 1937.

58. *Journal,* 1889, p. 23.

Chapter 3

Stretching Resources

1898 — 1922

It was June, 1898 when the Rev. Walter J. Smith, his wife and seven children left their home in Scotland Neck and moved to South Davidson Street in Charlotte. At the request of Joseph Cheshire, Bishop of the Diocese of North Carolina and chairman of the orphanage Board of Managers, Walter Smith had given up his position as rector of Trinity Parish, and the only home he had known in his 45 years, to become the second superintendent of the Thompson Orphanage.

The problems he inherited varied in degree from the almost inescapable mud which layered the campus, to the more serious problems of inadequate space for the children, no running water, insufficient heat, buildings which constantly needed repair, and the never-ending challenge of raising enough money to pay the bills.

As he explained in his first report to the Board of Managers:

> Eleven years' wear and tear on an institution like this is apt to show itself in many ways, and it is natural that a new comer should see many things which would escape the observation of a long resident, and so I have made such repairs and improvements here and there as seemed necessary, and consistent with the condition of our treasury. Fortunately, Mr. Osborne left funds on hand with which to do this work.[1]

The first major improvement was having water run to the orphanage in 1899. The cost for adding running water, about $700 to $800, was covered by funds raised at the 1898 Convention of the Diocese of North Carolina held in Henderson. Board members agreed this was "one of the greatest needs of the Institution, and will not only be a great convenience and lighten a heavy burden upon the Matrons and children, but will add to their comfort and health, and also to the safety of the buildings against fire."[2]

At about the same time a dining hall and infirmary were added to Bronson Hall, also built with funds collected at the previous year's Convention. The infirmary was furnished through contributions from the children of the Church, collected by "Aunt Becky" Cameron and given in memory of Benjamin Bronson's wife Alice Somerville Bronson.

Yet another improvement was the addition of telephone service which, affirmed Smith, "has proved to be a great convenience in the transaction of the business of the Institution, as well as in giving more prompt attention to the sick."[3]

At the turn of the century, there were 62 children living at the Thompson Orphanage: 33 from the Diocese of North Carolina, 24 from the Diocese of East Carolina, and five from the Missionary District of Asheville, representing an increase of 24 per cent over the previous year's enrollment. And although contributions to the orphanage did not increase in like amount, the Board commended Walter Smith for his "wise and judicious management" of available funds[4] and for the condition of the institution's financial records, "clearly and beautifully kept."[5]

A GROWING LIST OF NEEDS

The new superintendent was astute in business matters and had quickly taken on the practical, pressing challenge of raising adequate financial support for the institution, while stretching to the limit its resources. Shortly after his arrival he hired a Miss Whitaker to travel throughout North Carolina to raise funds for the orphanage and he made pragmatic use of his position as editor and manager of the diocesan newspaper *Messenger of Hope* to publicize orphanage events and needs, giving church members every opportunity to respond accordingly. In October, 1909, the *Messenger of Hope* was replaced with *The Carolina Churchman*, official newspaper of the Diocese of North Carolina, with Walter Smith as editor of the Thompson Orphanage Department.

He included in each newspaper's monthly issue a list of all contributors and donations received. Every gift, whether a few pennies or many dollars, was acknowledged, as well as in-kind contributions of clothing, food, bedding, utensils, farm implements, fuel and other supplies. The superintendent left nothing to chance when it came to opportunities for giving, providing explicit instructions for mailing a box of goods to the orphanage:

> 1. Fill it with useful articles worth more than the freight. 2. Fasten it securely and send by mail the list of contents and railroad receipt. 3. Do not put in any fire-crackers,

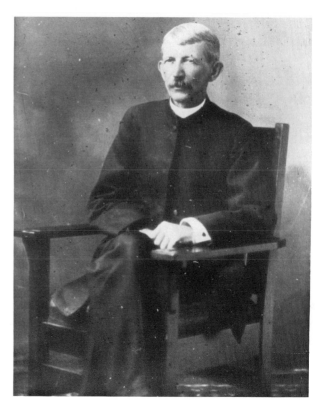

Walter J. Smith

chewing gum, baby shoes, baby caps, or worn-out clothes. 4. We need all kinds of food, strong cloth, spool thread, shoes above no.1, school books and good books, etc.[6]

Specific needs were also spelled out: "a few bed springs and mattresses and a bureau for the large girls' room in Thompson Hall"[7] and "some good ropes for swings — some that will not wear out so easily."[8]

A compassionate disciplinarian with the children, Smith was less tolerant with potential donors when it came to raising money.

> Look at the list for the first half of the month! Only sixteen dollars! About enough to take care of two children for a month! And yet each child gets his four biscuits for supper whether flour is high or low, or whether there is any money in the treasury or not. Now is the time for our sympathetic friends to send in a little cash to show their faith by their works.[9]

"AUNT BECKY" AND THE MESSENGERS OF HOPE

"Aunt Becky" Cameron of Hillsborough was one who did show her faith by works, soliciting support for the orphanage children from their more fortunate counterparts in Episcopal Sunday Schools across the state. It was through this network that funds were first raised for the Bishop Atkinson Memorial Cot Fund, transferred from its original St. John's Hospital destination to the Thompson Orphanage in 1893. The 'Messengers of Hope' then collected $47 to purchase a campus bell for the orphanage in 1897, the bell which summoned more than a generation of Thompson Orphanage children to meals, school classes, and chapel.[10]

An "infirmary fund" began November 28, 1898 and by February 28, 1899, $52 had been raised by the children for repairs to the infirmary floor. Both Bronson Hall and the Williamson Infirmary were re-painted in April, 1900, thanks to $120 donated for the purpose from "Aunt Becky" and the 'Messengers of Hope,' also known as the Junior Thompson Orphanage Guild. They then turned their efforts toward raising the entire amount of the orphanage sewing teacher's salary, $150 a year from 1900 to 1910 and up to $180 a year by 1911, a sum Miss Cameron admitted was, "beggarly little for a whole year's work."[11]

Joining the 'Messengers of Hope' in April, 1900 was a girl who for six years had been on the receiving end of the group's work. Her letter to "Aunt Becky" appeared in the *Messenger of Hope*:

> I am a new comer, and wish to help you in your great undertaking. I was myself one of the children at the Orphanage for six years, and know what a lovely home it is for fatherless and motherless children. I can truly say that the Orphanage is the best home for orphans that I have ever known. I have lived there and know it well. I love it dearly, and when I left it in the summer, I felt as if I was leaving a very dear friend behind me. I have heard people speak of an Orphanage as if it was something horrible to be at one, but I tell you it is a blessing to be at one.[12]

The writer's name ws not printed in the newspaper, although Miss Cameron appeared to know her well.

> I am delighted, dear child, to have you speak so gratefully and appreciatively of the home that sheltered you helpless children, when the Lord, by His mysterious dispensation, took from you in one week's time, both father and mother, leaving eight children helpless and unprovided. Your father was one of the most excellent of men; one of the humblest Christians. I held him in highest esteem from years of correspondence, for he was a most faithful and liberal contributor to the Messenger work from the very first. I think with you, that it is a blessing to have a home provided for helpless children, and I am always glad to do anything I can to help to provide for its support.[13]

"Aunt Becky" was as lavish with her praise as she was peppery in her scolding when it seemed a young contributor could do more: "Your last contribution my dear young lady was received on the 29th of March, which seems a rather long gap, does it not?"[14] Again frustrated with the pace of giving, she remarked in 1909, "The snail and the tortoise and the sloth are the lightning express compared with our progress."[15]

Ever on the alert for new money-making tactics, she suggested the children form "dollar clubs" and make money by "teas and hayrides, and similar entertainments."[16] The children responded with ideas of their own.

> Our Junior Auxiliary at our last meeting proposed a plan for raising money which we thought perhaps the other Juniors would like to adopt. We are going to ask each member of the church in our parish to subscribe five cents a month for Thompson Orphanage, which we will collect monthly, and if all the other Branches of the Diocese would do the same we might raise a sum large enough to be a real help . . . We are still selling our candy and put some of the money in our mite chests, but have decided always to send most of it to the Orphanage.[17]

> I am sending you in this letter twenty-five cents in stamps for Sewing Teacher's salary. I made it bringing in wood and picking up chips for my mother and wanted to send it to you for the little orphans. I am a little girl six years old and live at Tar River, eight miles from Oxford. There are no little church girls in this neighborhood, and as its too far to go to Oxford to be a member of the Junior Auxiliary, I can't contribute through that so will have to have a little society of my own. I hope to make some more money for next month and send for the poor little orphans.[18]

A Sunday School child's mother wrote to "Aunt Becky" in 1909, illustrating her daughter's commitment to help support the Thompson Orphanage: "She is always eager for her five cents for 'Aunt Becky's Sunday,' as we call the second Sunday in each month."[19]

Rebecca Cameron's work with the children was expanded upon by a vote in the Convention of the Diocese of North Carolina in May, 1911: Resolved that, "The plan of taking a monthly offering from each Sunday School be emphasized and extended, and that each clergyman bring this matter before his Sunday School at once."[20] Though not a rich source of monetary support, the Sunday School children were an important stimulus for giving by others within the church. "We must remember that these gifts and letters to 'Aunt Becky' are training the children in practical church work," explained Walter Smith.[21] "Go and do thou likewise," he encouraged other parishes and Sunday Schools in 1911.[22]

THE CHARACTER OF ORPHANAGE LIFE

Although electricity had been available in Charlotte as early as 1887, big coal stoves and kerosene lamps were still commonplace at the Thompson Orphanage even after 1900.[23] Physical improvements came slowly during the first decade of the new century, limited by shortages of cash to only the most practical additions. "A concrete floor, a bath tub and three shower baths"[24] were put in the boys' bathroom in Thompson Hall, and another bathroom and bath tub added in Bronson Hall. A concrete floor, three stationary washtubs and a water heater were installed in the wooden laundry building adjacent to Thompson Hall, and the school room was divided in half by partitions. The old dining room in Thompson Hall was converted to a family room with a new floor and "neat and comfortable wainscoting."[25]

Despite a sparsity of physical amenities, the children at the orphanage appeared to adapt and even thrive, their days filled with a routine of work, school studies, chapel services, and some recreation. Looking back on the era, Josephine Osborne insisted, "While this picture represents that their lives were plain, and perhaps a little hard, yet these young people seemed rather to increase than to lose in cheerfulness and spontaneity."[26]

The children attended school in half-day seg-

ments so they could also take care of their household and farm duties. Midday bells summoned everyone to the chapel for a short service, followed by the call to lunch.[27] "We used to grab a hat in one hand and a prayer book in the other", said former Thompson Orphanage resident Eva Bland Roberts, remembering those daily chapel services.

> Birds were always roosting on the chapel and annoying the minister with their cries. "Rev. Smith would interrupt the service and say, 'Will some of you boys go out and shoo the birds off the church.'"[28]

Every child was expected to help with assigned duties, the older girls doing laundry, dishes, cooking, preserving fruits and vegetables, ironing, mending, or helping with younger children, and the older boys responsible for keeping the fires going in winter, making trips to the ice house in summer, and always, tending to farm chores. Farming was considered an essential element of orphanage life, producing food for the table and training for the boys. The newspaper, *Charity and Children* of The Baptist Childrens' Homes, commended the role of institutional farming in an editorial November 10, 1904:

> The Orphanage farm is after all the most valuable department of the Institution, not only because of the revenue it produces but because it gives the boys an opportunity to be of some account in the world. Every orphanage ought to be located in the country and own a big farm.[29]

The intensity of the children's work regimen was most often visible in their clothes, as explained by the superintendent in 1909:

> . . . did you ever stop to consider how many clothes seventy children (especially those who work) can wear out, tear up and lose in a month, or how many shoes seventy pairs of feet can kick out in the same length of time? Yes, we do need clothing, especially jackets and pants for the boys, and shoes for all. Then too, we would like to have some material for the sewing room to make up into dresses for the girls and shirtwaists for the boys.[30]

When the farm produce came in, the children drove a donkey cart through town to sell the vegetables, and sometimes to gather up donations of leftover food or other items from local stores and restaurants. In the Spring of 1910, however, the faithful donkey died, prompting superintendent Smith to pen an eight-verse poem called, "The Donkey Is Dead," which he hoped would encourage contributions toward the purchase of another animal.

"The donkey is dead!" came over the 'phone
On a clear, cold morning like the frigid zone.
"The donkey is dead," with sorrow be it said,
And she died, it is true, of being overfed.

All day long she stood in her stall,
With nothing to do, with nothing to haul,
And as the boys passed by in playful mood,
They would toss her bits of extra food.

So after many days it came to pass
That for too much corn and too little grass,
She finally lost the power of locomotion,
In spite of hard rubbing and every kind of lotion.

The farmer and the boys at times stood around,
And did all they could to raise her from the ground,
But all their efforts proved to be in vain,
And she died, it seemed, without any pain.

The donkey and boys with their low wheel cart,
Of the Orphanage have formed a real true part;
For though she was but an humble creature,
The work she did was no small feature.

Time and again with two little boys,
With slower speed and much less noise
Back and forth she anon made her round,
To carry and fetch whatever was found.

Sometimes it was clothes and sometimes toys
To bring to the children many new joys.
Now who will give us another to take her place,
To make the same trips with the same slow pace?

Twenty-five dollars will about do it,
And if you give it you will never rue it.
So out with your purse, and down with the cash,
And no one will say the deed is rash.

Response was not as lively as the rhyme.

Dear Juniors (Jr. Auxiliary): How many of you recall a poem Rev. W.J. Smith of the Thompson Orphanage wrote last winter entitled, 'The Donkey Is Dead'? Mr. Smith writes that the donkey is still dead and that the fund for a new one grows very slowly. This patient beast is very needful for the young folks at the Orphanage. Cannot one Junior send in some money for a new one, so that by September 1st, 'the orphans' may be harvesting and marketing their crops with his assistance? Lets give a long pull and a strong pull and pull a new donkey, no matter how stubborn he may be, from someone's pasture. Kate Shepherd Bennett, Sec. J. Aux. Com., Charlotte.[31]

By the end of the year they had a donkey, sending it for its first trip after a coop of turkeys donated to the orphanage by J.G. Shannonhouse.[32]

GEJOGGLING AND MUD-SLINGING

While the practicalities of orphanage life required the children to work and study, the institution was not a workhouse. The front lawn of the orphanage was a popular spot for a variety of games such as shooting marbles, skipping rope, pitching horseshoes or whirling on the merry-go-round called by the children "the ocean wave."[33] In September, 1910, the superintendent reported in the diocesan newspaper, "The large girls and little children enjoyed a gejoggling board given by J.H. Wearn & Co., of Charlotte, till the big boys jumped on it and broke it."[34] When they weren't getting into similar mischief, the boys played on the orphanage baseball team.

Sugar Creek was dredged and widened between September — October, 1911 to help alleviate the constant flooding across the campus lowland, and gravel was brought up from orphanage property to fill in the walkways, cutting down considerably on 'mud-slinging,' another popular entertainment among the boys.

The children often received free tickets to local movie houses, the circus, and traveling fairs. The Thompson Orphanage Guild at St. Peter's Church sponsored an Easter egg hunt each year, as well as most of the food, decorations and gifts for the Thanksgiving and Christmas feasts. Traditionally, the Christmas celebration began with a service in the chapel, followed by a dinner which lacked nothing, including "oysters and mince pie."[35] Then with the windows in the schoolroom darkened and candles lighted, the

Thompson Orphanage's country setting invited outdoor games

children would march in singing "Hark! The Herald Angels Sing" or "Shout the Glad Tidings." In addition to gifts underneath the tree, each child received a bag from its branches containing nuts, candy and fruit.

The orphans, in turn, expressed gratitude to their benefactors as often as possible, although not always in as unique a fashion as they did on New Year's Eve, 1909. Accompanied by the superintendent, a group of orphanage children delivered a wreath of funeral flowers to the West Trade Street residence of Judge William Preston Bynum, the man who had donated funds for St. Mary's Chapel. On New Year's Day about half the children went to his funeral and received, according to the terms of Bynum's will, two dollars each for their attendance. The Judge also left $1,000 in unrestricted funds to Thompson Orphanage.[36]

In summer, many of the children left the campus to visit friends or relatives, but those who remained were given a picnic, such as the one described by Walter Smith in 1911, held at Charlotte's Lakewood Park:

Laughing, talking and singing, the merry crowd had a delightful ride to the park, and . . . went first to the pavilion to get a good view of the beautiful lake, and then they scattered around beneath the trees, some of them of course rushing for the water pipes to test the virtues of the 'pure spring water' as compared with the liquid that trickles slowly along the bottom of Irwin's creek. A few fortunate ones who possessed a little change invested it in peanuts and ice cream, and soon all were gathered with eager interest around the merry-go-round on which the proprietor, Mr. Bradshaw, the pleasant manager, kindly gave them a free ride. From there they made a visit to the genial operator of the roller coaster, Mr. Church. He, too, had a tender spot in his heart for the orphans and soon the cars were being packed with happy and smiling children, half eager and half afraid. Nearly every one rode the gauntlet, even little George Williams, the baby pet of the Orphanage, who was hugged up closely in Ivie Smith's arms. Last, but not least, the obliging Mr. Roper gave them a ride round the lake on the gasoline yacht. Counting the crew, there were even fifty persons on board, and as the sweet voices of the children were wafted over the placid waters all went 'merry as a marriage bell.'[37]

A GOOD INFLUENCE

While life at Thompson Orphanage was not always "merry as a marriage bell," it had a profound effect on the children. And Walter Smith was eager to point to appropriate examples, such as Mary and Victor who "after a bath, change of clothing and a hair cut" on the day of their arrival in February, 1910, "did not look like the same beings."[38] After only a month at Thompson Orphanage the children were "fat and rosy . . . and well satisfied with their new home."[39]

The influence of a Thompson Orphanage upbringing was often recognized, and appreciated, after children left the home. In a letter to his former matron in February, 1910, one of the 'old boys' in the U.S. Coast Guard revealed, "The words of Mr. Osborne and Mr. Smith and of the matrons and teachers at the Orphange often recur to me as I go about my duty, and they invariably have a good influence over my conduct . . . For this kindly advice and counsel I shall ever feel grateful to the faculty of the Thompson Orphanage."[40]

Others could also see a difference in children after they had been in the orphanage.

A brother clergyman, who is a good supporter of the Orphanage, writing of one of our girls now on a visit home, says, 'She has shown great improvement and is a bright witness of the benefit and influence of the training received there;' and another brother, equally as faithful, is kind enough to say, 'Verily the children of the Thompson Orphanage reflect the training they get, as one cannot fail to note the improvement after they have been in the orphanage.'[41]

The pervading attitude at Thompson Orphanage during these first years of the twentieth century was that of simplicity. The common virtues were extolled, and practiced: truthfulness, punctuality, reliability, good manners, ability to follow instructions and good cheer.[42] It was not inappropriate that the address to the children at the 1911 school closing exercises was "The Value of the Commonplace in Life." Speaking to the students, the Rev. F.J. Mallett of St. Luke's Church, Salisbury explained "this is the age of the common man . . . and so today we must cultivate an appreciation of common blessings, common men, for as Lincoln said,

'God must love the common people, because He made so many of them.' "He challenged the students to "cultivate from earliest days these sterling common-sense virtues."[43]

As if in affirmation, the closing program included, among the 'motion songs' and recitations, a lively 'Patriotic Drill' by 16 of the orphanage girls.

SHARING IDEAS

The Thompson Orphanage, up to this point, had not progressed in isolation, but was part of a growing number of private orphanages established across North Carolina and the South. Despite the government's pledge in the Constitution of 1868, the state of North Carolina never established nor fully funded an orphanage,[44] leaving residential care of orphans almost entirely to religious organizations, in particular the Episcopal, Baptist, Presbyterian, Catholic and Methodist churches. And there was no dearth of applicants for any of the institutions.

This was a period of high mortality, morbidity, and accident rates of parents, especially fathers; of limited access to medical care; of a paucity of preventive health services; and an almost total absence of welfare services. The resulting number of orphaned children far exceeded the facilities available to care for them.

The superintendents of these various institutions often shared experiences and visited other campuses to discover more efficient, and effective, methods of care. In the March, 1910 edition of the *Carolina Churchman*, Walter Smith reported, " . . . we left the next morning for Barium Springs Orphanage where we received every courtesy from the officials in charge . . . We often gather from such visits both suggestions and encouragement in our own work."[46]

The Tri-State (North Carolina, South Carolina and Georgia) Conference of Orphanage Workers, organized in 1904, held its annual convention in Charlotte April 18-20, 1911, enabling many of its members to visit the Thompson Orphanage. After a ride on Charlotte's electric streetcar from convention headquarters at the YMCA, conference members toured the orphanage and were treated to ice cream and cake served by the orphans and members of the Thompson Orphanage Guild. Conference business sessions were opened with singing led by a choir of boys and girls from Thompson Orphanage.

Among the topics presented at the 1911 conference were "Educational and Industrial Standards in Orphanage Work," "Orphanage Financiering," and "The Orphanage Farm." The Rev. A.T. Jamison, superintendent of the Connie Maxwell Orphanage in Greenville, S.C. tied together the goals of the various institutions in his address, "The Christian Obligation in Orphanage Work." In response, Dr. Cole of the Methodist Orphanage in Raleigh said: "I believe that we have been a happier people ever since we entered this field of benevolence . . . This work we are doing is the greatest blessing that has come to the State of North Carolina in my time."[47]

In his address on "The Wayward Boy," Walter Thompson of the Jackson Training School emphasized the importance of intense individual attention for such boys, a point reinforced by William Laurie Hill of Barium Springs Orphange who commented, "A good woman has the best influence over a large boy."[48]

THE JOB OF A GOOD WOMAN

The 'good woman' at the Thompson Orphanage was the matron who had almost uninterrupted charge of 'wayward boys' and girls alike. The matron was expected to fill many roles: housekeeper, seamstress, cook, nurse, teacher, mother, friend. Even though others were gradually hired to take over some of these specific duties, such as sewing and housecleaning, the ultimate responsibility for each cottage, and the behavior of the children in it, fell to the matron.

Elizabeth J. Mackay, the first orphanage matron, announced her retirement in May, 1900 "on account of the work becoming too heavy for her strength,"[49] but was persuaded to stay on until April, 1902. "Under conditions that were crowded, and facilities unbelievably scanty, her stalwart character and marvelous integrity and good judgement wrought upon the raw material, and developed them into fine young men and women,"[50] recalled Josephine Osborne. Within the next eight years there were five different matrons at Thompson Hall, before the arrival in 1910 of Mrs. T.J. Wooldridge of Richmond, who became a stable influence on the older children in her care. Matrons for Bronson Hall were

"Rena" Mackay, who died in 1892, Mrs. M.P. Prentiss, Mrs. Sargent, and finally Miss Kate Capehart who, in 1911, was beginning her twentieth year in the position.

Kate Capehart

School teachers, too, had considerable influence on the lives of the orphanage children. Together with the matrons, teachers were required to attend the daily chapel services, and to teach in the Sunday School. Miss Lily May Tomlin, primary teacher from 1908 to 1911, led the choir and played the organ in the chapel. Josephine Osborne, daughter of the first superintendent, taught during the 1899-1900 school year, remarking later, "As has ever been true of the young people here, my students were most courteous and responsive."[51] "Essie" Call, a former student who had received much of her education at Thompson Orphanage, returned between 1910-1911 to teach the primary department. She had come to the orphanage in June, 1888 at the age of 11. At the opening of the 1911-1912 school year, Mrs. Sarah E. Hanks had charge of the seniors, and Mrs. Harold N. Clare the juniors.

The school was divided into senior and primary (or junior) departments, each requiring a full-time teacher who lived on the campus, sharing the residence buildings with the children and matrons. In the classroom, teachers rewarded all manner of achievement, presenting prizes at the end of each school year for Scholarship, Improvement in Penmanship, Good Behavior, Improvement in Sewing, and four in 1911 received their board plus $45 a month.

Salaries for other orphanage staff that year ranged from less than $60 a month for farm foreman Ernest Jamison, who lived in a cottage on the grounds, to $40 a month plus board for the Thompson Hall housekeeper, Miss Lou Hall Hill. Since Thompson Hall was larger and housed more children, its matron made $50 a month, the Bronson Hall matron a monthly salary of $45. Miss E. Belle Field, sewing teacher, made $40 a month.[53] Charlotte physicians and dentists, as they had since the founding of the orphanage, provided their services free of charge. The first orphanage physician in 1886 was Dr. Simmons B. Jones, followed by several others until 1908 when Dr. William Myers Hunter took over the position which he held, except for time served in WW I, for 32 years.

In addition to low wages and hard work, Thompson Orphanage staff members had to abide by regulations as strict as those imposed on the children. It took an action of the Executive Committee in October, 1906 to decide that teachers and matrons should sit at the same table with the children. In April, 1909 the Board of Managers ordered that the matrons and other employees could not leave the grounds without the consent of the superintendent and that both matrons should not be absent at the same time. Though staff members complained about the rigid rules, the Board stood firm on its decision, yielding only slightly in April, 1911 saying the superintendent, remembered equally for his gentleness and firm belief in discipline, should use his judgement in interpreting the rules.

THE FEDERATION OF ORPHANAGE GUILDS

From the earliest days of Thompson Orphanage, the women of the church proved a reliable source of support for the staff of the institution. The first Thompson Orphanage Guild was formed at St. Peter's Church in Charlotte, its nine members pledging to support one child, then quickly broadening that pledge "until it included any need which Mr. Osborne requested."[54]

Guild members in Charlotte saw themselves as "forsworn to uphold the holy cause. If that cause were clothes a call to arms was sounded and soon they met together at some home and fell to cutting and stitching until this need was vanquished.[55] They also provided food, donated paint to brighten walls, made curtains, and treated the children to parties, picnics and special trips. To raise money, members staged plays, sponsored teas, concerts, and suppers, and held sales "of all things salable", proclaiming "it matters not how the funds are raised, taking for granted that it is by honest work or honest begging."[56]

In 1906, Walter Smith encouraged the Charlotte guild to take the lead in forming a chain of women's groups across the state to be called the Federation of Thompson Orphanage Guilds. At its October 27, 1906 meeting, the orphanage Executive Committee acknowledged the idea, noting that St. Peter's proposed to send out an agent representing the Federation to help organize guilds, "solicit contributions for the current expenses of the orphanage and for a special Building Fund for the erection of a new building or buildings." That agent was Miss Emma Joy Hall.

A perfectionist of dogged determination, Emma Hall was indefatigable in her efforts to organize the Federation. In each of the five years between 1906 and 1911 she traveled the state, "telling the story of the Orphanage to all who would hear . . . seeking to organize Guilds where possible and to create an interest in everything pertaining to this Institution which is so dear to the hearts of all of us."[57] Joining the Federation were guilds from Raleigh, Scotland Neck, Wadesboro, Salisbury, Concord, Oxford, Henderson, Tarboro, Wilmington, Winston-Salem, Greensboro, Asheville, Gastonia, Edenton, Rockingham, and the Church of the Holy Comforter in Charlotte.

A "THOROUGHLY MODERN" GOAL

Almost immediately the Federation set as its singular vision to raise $100,000 for a "thoroughly modern and hygienically constructed set of buildings on the 'Cottage System', now generally conceded to be the best for institutional work."[58] The plan included a main building with school rooms, gymnasium and central heating plant, an infirmary, a home for the superintendent, and six brick cottages, each designed to house between 16 and 24 children and a matron. Yet there seemed controversy about the plan from the very first.

In the November, 1909 issue of the *Carolina Churchman*, Charlotte guild members described conditions at the orphanage as they saw them: "The children housed and fed by us are improperly housed and improperly fed because the facilities are lacking — in tottering and unhygienic walls—for properly housing or properly feeding a growing child."

While acknowledging the need for improvements, Superintendent Smith responded in the next edition:

> It is true that the walls of the old original building are crumbling to pieces, and that that part of the building is not in a sanitary condition, but the new additions made by the former superintendent are built with first class brick, and well put up. The lower dormitory for the boys is 16×20 feet, and has four windows. It accommodates nine boys. The upper dormitory has eleven boys in it, and is 16×24 with even better ventilation. The girls dormitories are equally spacious and substantial, though not so well ventilated. Bronson Hall, the other building, for a wooden structure answers its purpose very well. We do need a new building and we hope it will soon come, but the first consideration is to feed and clothe the children . . . [59]

It was agreed, however, that improvements and new buildings were needed. On April 27, 1910, the Board of Managers called a special meeting of its building committee at the Charlotte home of Federation President Mrs. Vinton Liddell to view preliminary plans and a sketch of the proposed first cottage prepared by local architect Louis Asbury. Members of the building committee were the Rt. Rev. Joseph Cheshire, Bishop of the Diocese of North Carolina and chairman of the Board of Managers, Walter J. Smith, superintendent, and orphanage attorney Joseph G. Shannonhouse. The final member of the committee was Edwin Osborne who, following the Spanish-American War, had been assigned to St. Mary's School in Raleigh as chaplain before returning to Charlotte in 1900 as Archdeacon of the Convocation of Charlotte.

The building committee authorized the Federation to perfect the plans and get building cost estimates, but cautioned against directing all guild efforts toward the buildings at the risk of neglecting the daily needs of the orphanage.

In subsequent meetings, the committee suggested a number of changes in the original design including a wide piazza, basement storage and additional second-floor rooms, agreeing to assume the additional costs necessary. On May 11, 1911 the committee withdrew its requirements, "owing to the disagreement between the building committee and the Committee of the Federation of Guilds".[60] Committee members authorized the Federation to proceed with the cottage, to be built between the two existing halls, but warned if it should prove unsatisfactory, the matter of the other changes would again be considered for any other cottages.

More space was desperately needed with the climbing number of applications for admission each year. In the Fall of 1911 there were 67 children crowded into the orphanage which, observed the superintendent, "is neither an omnibus nor an India rubber house",[61] to be stretched beyond its capacity.

The cornerstone for the long-awaited Federation Cottage was laid in an elaborate ceremony on April 23, 1912. Superintendent Smith placed a number of articles in the cornerstone, including a Bible, the Episcopal Prayer Book, the October, 1911, edition of *The Carolina Churchman* which contained a short history of the institution, and that day's *Charlotte Daily Observer* with the leading headline, "Sea Gives Up 53 of Titanic's Dead".[62]

In 1913, while Federation Cottage was under construction, another building was added to the campus: a home for the superintendent, built with funds from the legacy of J.C. Stedman of Fayetteville and called Stedman Hall.

Federation Cottage was completed in 1914, "with every convenience, even luxury of a modern three-story brick and stone home . . . with mission furniture made at Kanuga and donated by Mrs. George Stephens."[63] Mrs. Stephens was the daughter of John Springs Myers, whose 1,100-acre plantation was developed by son-in-law George Stephens in 1910 as the Myers Park community.[64] The Junior Thompson Orphanage Guild supplied iron beds and bedclothes for each child, with table linens and towels from the guild at All Saint's Church in Concord. The "children's guild" gave "a wonderful base burner capable of heating the whole cottage" and the senior guild "supplied all the other furnishings from the range to crockery . . . "[65]

Shortly after the cottage opened, the Federation of Thompson Orphanage Guilds disbanded, due in large part to the outbreak of World War I which curtailed the members' ability to travel and diverted their efforts toward war-related needs.

ADMISSIONS AND CHALLENGES MULTIPLY

With Federation Cottage open, more children could be accepted at the orphanage. Among those who came in 1914 were 6-year old Ben Nash and his 4-year old brother Pat. "We came from a very poor family," explained Ben Nash.[66] The boys' mother, who worked in a five-and-dime store in Raleigh, couldn't make ends meet so through her affiliation with Christ Church, wrote Walter Smith asking that her sons be accepted at the orphanage. She put her boys on the train in Raleigh, each with tags around their necks advertising their destination as "Thompson Orphanage, Charlotte." One of the older orphanage boys, as was the custom, drove the donkey cart to the train station to meet the boys and bring them to their new home. It was a singular privilege, Nash discovered, to be in command of the wagon, or to be the boy selected to ride the donkey out to Newell each year to swap for a new one, though the inevitable saddle sores made it a mixed blessing.[67]

Grateful 'inmates' pose before Federation Cottage, later re-named Smith Cottage.

The Nash brothers were placed in Thompson Hall where, admitted Ben Nash, "we just stuck it out with the big boys."[68] The younger boys slept in the upstairs dormitory, the older ones downstairs. "It was up to the matrons to take care of us."[69] However, when it came to discipline, "Mr. Smith didn't mind at all" taking off his belt and using it, if a boy "stepped over the line".[70] Although life was hard, "we were normal kids growing up," recalled Nash. "We just had a lot of farm work. I milked four cows twice a day for 12 years!"[71]

Increased dormitory space in the orphanage also meant more children in the school. To help alleviate overcrowding, the Board of Managers voted to send some of the children to Charlotte's public schools, beginning in the Fall of 1916. It was a move which had been considered since as early as 1908 and was encouraged by a report

from H.P. Harding, superintendent of Charlotte's public schools, affirming that orphanage children would be "permitted" to attend. Thompson Orphanage was one of the first institutions in the South to send its children off campus to public schools.

Despite its many improvements, the institution was beleaguered with reports of unsatisfactory physical conditions. A letter from John L. Jackson, rector of St. Martin's Church, Charlotte, and read into the minutes of the June 19, 1915 special Board of Managers meeting, contained "charges as to unsatisfactory conditions at the Orphanage as reported to the former by the Physician, Dr. Hunter."[72] The Executive Committee then asked the state's sanitary inspector to examine conditions at the orphanage during the remainder of June and July. No new admissions were accepted between June and the October 5, 1915 meeting of the Committee, where the inspector's report was received and nearly $1500 approved for necessary improvements to the buildings.

Among the items requiring attention were bathrooms and tubs in old Thompson Hall, and the kitchen and laundry at Bronson Hall deemed "dilapidated and totally unfit for such purposes."[73] The repairs in Thompson Hall, completed at the end of 1915, cost nearly $1,000. The Board of Managers, meeting in April, 1916 then approved the projects for Bronson Hall as well as resolving to build a new barn and an additional cottage for younger children ages two to seven years. Edwin Osborne was employed as Special Financial Agent to raise money for the proposed cottage and other improvements at a salary of $50 a month plus travel expenses.

Finally, in April, 1917, the Board appointed William S. Balthis, F.W. Glover, William G. Clark and William C. Ruffin as a committee to raise at least $50,000 for permanent improvements to the orphanage property.

DEATH OF BENJAMIN BRONSON

Even with its problems, the Thompson Orphanage property had improved vastly since its initial use as a boys' school between 1867 and 1873. The Rev. Benjamin Swan Bronson, whose generosity had allowed the property to come under the ownership of the Diocese of North Carolina, died in Warren County, N.C. on April 14, 1917 at the age of 89. He had watched the progress of Thompson Orphanage during the remainder of his ministry, having served at St. Timothy's in Wilson, the Church of the Good Shepherd in Rocky Mount, and finally opening another boys' school in Warrenton between 1897 and 1901.

ADMISSIONS POLICY

The condition of the campus buildings had little effect on the growing numbers of children recommended for admission each year. There were so many children needing care that the Board of Managers again examined the purpose for the orphange, and reiterated in April, 1917,

> . . . this institution was established for the express purpose of assuming permanent charge of the children committed to its care and keeping for the purpose of giving them moral, religious and practical training until they reach the age limit (16) heretofore decided upon.[74]

The following year the Board clarified its position on admissions stating that,

> . . . the object of the Orphanage is to provide a home for the orphan and destitute children of the State, selecting them according to the circumstances of the applicants without regard to their religious belongings, but giving the preference to the Church children, all other things being equal.[75]

In response to questions about the balance of children from the three areas of the state, the Board said children would be taken from each diocese "as far as practical, in proportion to the numerical strength of the respective jurisdictions."[76] In 1917 there were 74 children in the institution, 45 from the Diocese of North Carolina, 11 from East Carolina and 18 from the Missionary District of Asheville.

In general, the children remained healthy even if their physical surroundings were ailing. They bounced back from the normal childhood bumps, bruises, and occasional broken bones and diseases such as measles, whooping cough and even diphtheria. In 1919, however, there were five cases of tuberculosis reported. By November, 1919, two of the children had already returned to school and the others were listed as improving after "sleeping in the open and taking a special diet of milk, eggs and meat."[77] Partly because some cases still lingered into August, 1920, the Executive Committee ordered that all new applicants to the orphanage be given physical and mental tests before admission.

FINANCES

Salaries, building repairs and improvements, food, clothing and other essentials of daily life were a constant strain on the orphanage budget, a budget which leaned most heavily on the 'Thanksgiving Offering' taken in the state's Episcopal churches each year. It was an uncertain source of revenue at best, and the superintendent and Board of Managers often had to ask creditors for extensions on some of the heavier bills until after the November collection. In October, 1918, Walter Smith's report to the Executive Committee showed less than ten dollars in the orphanage treasury. As the same time the farm manager and other employees had asked for raises and funds were still needed for improvements such as repairs to the boys' dormitory steps. The new coat of paint due Bronson Hall that month was cancelled.

While the daily operating funds for the institution continued to fluctuate, an Endowment Fund set up May 1, 1900 helped build up some permanent reserves. The first trustee of the fund was Joseph G. Shannonhouse, who began service to the orphanage in 1886 as a member of the finance committee. At the end of its first year, the Endowment Fund had a balance of $2,389.75 and in 1917 it had grown to $19,278.98. Early in November, 1918 the institution borrowed $4,000 from its permanent funds "for the purpose of paying a pressing balance on ... contracts for improvements at the Orphanage ... "[78] including the new barn. By December, 1918, following receipt of the Thanksgiving Offering, the orphanage was able, "on account of the high cost of living," to raise foreman Ernest Jamison's salary to $18 a week.[79]

MORE NEW BUILDINGS PLEDGED

In November, 1919, the orphanage received a $10,000 legacy from Mrs. Sadie Tucker Williamson which, at the request of her husband William, was first set aside to build a cottage for the younger children. The next year Williamson agreed that the funds could be used to build a much-needed infirmary instead.

At the Convention of the Diocese of North Carolina, held in Charlotte in 1920, W.A. Erwin of Durham proposed building a cottage for the smaller children in honor of the first superintendent, Edwin Osborne, and by the following day enough subscriptions were pledged to begin the project.[80] A groundbreaking ceremony was held May 5, 1921, the eve of Edwin Osborne's 84th birthday and though it was completed by Fall, there was not enough furniture or equipment to open the Edwin A. Osborne Memorial Cottage until late in 1922.

In his annual report to the Board of Managers in January, 1922, Walter Smith was finally able to paint an improved financial picture for the orphanage, attributing much of it to "the fact that our people learned to give more liberally during the War."[81] After paying all the bills and investing in an $800 tenement house to be rented on the grounds, the orphanage still had $4000 over what it began with the previous year. The tenement house was built with old lumber from the laundry at Bronson Hall, torn down early in 1921.

A NEW SUPERINTENDENT

Even as the institution's financial health improved, the superintendent's physical health weakened. Walter Smith had never been particularly robust, and the pressures of managing the orphanage appear to have taken their toll on his stamina and enthusiasm. As early as 1915, during the state sanitary inspection and subsequent report on physical conditions, references appeared in the Board of Managers' minutes about seeking a "new superintendent." Minutes from the May 31, 1917 meeting of the Executive Committee proposed "that inasmuch as Mr. Smith expressed a willingness to resign his position as superintendent, his resignation be accepted to take effect January 1, 1918 ... " A number of men were considered for the position, but a suitable replacement could not be found and Walter Smith was re-elected superintendent on April 23, 1918 with a 10 per cent increase in salary.

The search for what the Executive Committee described as a "younger and more active man"[82] continued, however. On April 30, 1920, the Board of Managers hit upon an interim solution, electing Smith chaplain of the institution at his present salary and asking him to perform his duties as superintendent until another could be appointed. Ads for the position were placed in the *New York Churchman, The Living Church,* and the *Southern Churchman* until May, 1921, reading:

> WANTED: Layman for superintendent Church Orphange. Age 30 to 50. Preferably married. Qualifications— lover of children and experienced in business. Address Rev. E.A. Penick, Jr., Charlotte, N.C.[83]

Among the many people answering the ad was Miss Margaret M. Proffe, who had spent four months of her first sabbatical year of deaconess training at the Thompson Orphanage in the Spring of 1914. Although the assumption was that 'layman' referred to a man, Miss Proffe responded in her letter to the Rev. Edwin Penick, then rector of St. Peter's Church in Charlotte, "I know what I want when I see it."[84]

After considering many applicants, the Executive Committee met in a special session on June 21, 1922 to interview the Rev. William Hardin Wheeler of Wilmington, N.C., who had come with high recommendations from Bishop Thomas C. Darst of the Diocese of East Carolina. Wheeler and his family were on their way back to California after a term in Wilmington where he served since 1919 as rector of St. James Church. He had just stopped in Charlotte to observe the work of the Episcopal church at the orphanage, intending to continue on to California. He never completed the trip.

"Mr. Wheeler took dinner at the Orphanage and was shown over the grounds and buildings," by members of the Executive Committee.[85] Five days later he was officially offered the position of superintendent of the Thompson Orphanage and Training Institution at a salary of $2500 a year.

William H. Wheeler was a man of curious contradictions whose spare frame and kindly face belied his adventurous past in the rugged mining and logging camps of California's Sierra mountains. The son of a wealthy Hudson River Valley, N.Y. businessman, Wheeler had already shocked his family by shunning an entrepreneurial future to enter the Episcopal ministry. "They thought I'd gone astray," he remembered.[86]

After receiving his degree from the Church Divinity School of The Pacific in 1905, Wheeler was ordained deacon and priest in 1906 and sent, as he remembered it, "into the wilds of the Sierras," where he learned to straddle flat cars loaded with logs, and minister to mountain men who got "dead drunk" on payday.[87] He served two churches and traveled back and forth to various logging and mining camps in the area. In what he called his "only successful mining adventure" he went to Black Oak Mine to share the tenets of the church, and came back with the mine owner's daughter as his wife.[88]

In 1916 Wheeler took his family back to New York to be with his father during an illness, and while there served as rector of St. Andrew's Church, Beacon-on-the-Hudson, N.Y. He then moved South in 1919, to take over St. James Church in Wilmington, N.C., winning the admiration of Bishop Thomas Darst and setting in motion a chain of events which propelled him, like a jostling string of overloaded flat cars, to the doors of the Thompson Orphanage in 1922.

The "Roaring Twenties" had been ushered in and, in the eyes of the Orphanage Board, so had the appropriate man for the era.

The front lawn of Thompson Orphanage was alive with children intent on their last games of summer. It was September 1, and the 1922 school term was about to begin.

The boys scurried to get in just one more game of baseball while the girls, squealing and giggling, took refuge behind the prickly pines from the one who was 'it.' For days afterward it would be the subject of great argument as to who saw, or heard, it first. It came in a whirling dust cloud, with pings of spattering gravel and a low, contented purring. And at the wheel of his 'lizzie', sat the new superintendent, William H. Wheeler. His bright eyes drew up in creases as he smiled and waved to the children lined up along the driveway, close enough to satisfy curiosity yet back enough to jump out of the way if the car should make a sudden turn. Plenty of automobiles passed by the orphanage these days; few ever drove in, none stayed. At least, not until today.

The cloud settled in front of Stedman Cottage as Wheeler jerked to a stop in front of the superintendent's residence. He exhaled visably before climbing to the ground where a sea of childrens' bobbing heads greeted him. He stopped to gently touch each one.

The sun hung low in the sky, a brilliant orange arc stretching the length of the campus. Wheeler adjusted his collar, pushed the dust from his sleeves and stretched out his arms, circling the children around him on the front steps.

FOOTNOTES

1. *Journal,* 1899, p. 23.

2. Ibid., p. 22.

3. Ibid., p. 23.

4. Ibid., p. 22.

5. "Minutes," Board of Managers, May 1, 1900.

6. *The Messenger of Hope,* April, 1900, p. 1.

7. Ibid.

8. *The Carolina Churchman,* October, 1909, p. 16.

9. Ibid.

10. "What the Messengers of Hope Have Done," *The Carolina Churchman*, October, 1911, p. 22.

11. *The Carolina Churchman*, October, 1909, p. 17.

12. *The Messenger of Hope*, April, 1900, p. 1.

13. Ibid.

14. *The Carolina Churchman*, November, 1909, p. 17.

15. *The Carolina Churchman*, December, 1909, p. 17.

16. *The Carolina Churchman* October, 1909, p. 17.

17. *The Messenger of Hope*, April, 1900, p. 1.

18. *The Carolina Churchman*, October, 1909, p. 17.

19. *The Carolina Churchman*, November, 1909, p. 17.

20. "Sunday Schools and the Orphanage," *The Carolina Churchman*, October, 1911, p. 22.

21. *The Carolina Churchman*, January, 1910, p. 20.

22. *The Carolina Churchman*, October, 1911, p. 22.

23. Josephine Osborne to Dr. Milton Barber, February 5, 1937.

24. *The Carolina Churchman*, October, 1911, p. 8.

25. *The Messenger of Hope*, April, 1900, p. 3.

26. Josephine Osborne, "Reminiscence," prepared for Thompson Orphanage Semi-Centennial Jubilee, May 7, 1937.

27. Ibid.

28. Hannah Miller, "Thompson Graduates Return To Orphanage For Reunion," *The Charlotte Observer*, June 25, 1962, p. 1B.

29. Fink, p. 350.

30. *The Carolina Churchman*, December, 1909, p. 16.

31. *The Carolina Churchman*, August, 1910, p. 16.

32. *The Carolina Churchman*, December, 1910, p. 16.

33. Hannah Miller, "Thompson Graduates Return," p.

34. *The Carolina Churchman*, September, 1910, p. 13.

35. *The Carolina Churchman*, February, 1910, p. 16.

36. Ibid.

37. "Happy Orphans at Lakewood Park," *The Carolina Churchman*, October, 1911, p. 25.

38. *The Carolina Churchman*, March, 1910, p. 16.

39. Ibid.

40. "A Word From One of Our Old boys," *The Carolina Churchman*, March, 1910, p. 17.

41. *The Carolina Churchman*, September, 1910, p. 13.

42. "Closing Exercises of the School," *The Carolina Churchman*, October, 1911, p. 24.

43. Ibid.

44. Fink, p. 339.

45. Ibid.

46. *The Carolina Churchman*, March, 1910, p. 6.

47. "The Tri-State Conference of Orphanage Workers," *The Carolina Churchman*, May, 1911, p. 15.

48. Ibid.

49. "Minutes," Board of Managers, May 1, 1900.

50. Josephine Osborne, "Reminiscence," May 7, 1937.

51. Ibid.

52. "Closing Exercises," *The Carolina Churchman*, October, 1911, pp. 24-25.

53. Walter J. Smith, an undated note on Thompson Orphanage stationery, Thompson Orphanage Historical Files, Charlotte, N.C.

54. "The Federation of Thompson Orphanage Guilds," *The Carolina Churchman*, October, 1911, p. 8.

55. Ibid., p. 9.

56. *The Carolina Churchman*, March, 1910, p. 17.

57. *The Carolina Churchman*, June, 1910, p. 6.

58. *The Carolina Churchman*, October, 1911, p. 9.

59. *The Carolina Churchman*, December, 1909, p. 16.

60. "Minutes," Thompson Orphanage Building Committee, May 11, 1911.

61. *The Carolina Churchman*, November, 1911, p. 17.

62. Dot Jackson, "Stone Hid Past's Relics," *The Charlotte Observer*, June 3, 1970, p. 1B.

63. Mrs. Louis Burwell, "Charitable and Humane Institutions" *The Charlotte News*, Young Women's Christian Association Edition, May 26, 1914, p. 14.

64. Kratt, p. 118.

65. Ibid.

66. Ben Nash, interview, April 10, 1985.

67. Ibid.

68. Ibid.

69. Ibid.

70. Ibid.

71. Ibid.

72. "Minutes," Board of Managers, June 19, 1915.

73. "Minutes," Executive Committee, August 21, 1914.

74. "Minutes," Board of Managers, April, 1917.

75. "Minutes," Executive Committee, July 9, 1918.

76. Ibid.

77. "Special Report of the Executive Committee," November 17, 1919.

78. Joseph G. Shannonhouse to Edwin A. Osborne, November 2, 1918, Thompson Orphanage Historical Files, Charlotte, N.C.

79. "Minutes," Executive Committee, December 13, 1918.

80. "The Building For Small Children at the Thompson Orphanage and Training Institution," August 15, 1922, Thompson Orphanage Historical Files, Charlotte, N.C.

81. "Annual Report of the Superintendent of the Thompson Orphanage and Training Instutition," January, 1922, p. 1. (Hereinafter cited as "Annual Report.")

82. "Minutes," Executive Committee, February 10, 1920.

83. Edwin A. Penick to Joseph G. Shannonhouse, August 21, 1920, Edwin A. Penick Papers, Thompson Orphanage, 1920-1949, Diocesan House, Raleigh, N.C.

84. Margaret M. Proffe to Edwin A. Penick, September 9, 1920, Edwin A. Penick Papers, Thompson Orphanage, 1920-1949, Diocesan House, Raleigh, N.C.

85. "Minutes," Executive Committee, June 21, 1922.

86. Hannah Miller, "He Rode Flat Cars In Logging Camps," undated newspaper clipping circa 1962, Thompson Orphanage Historical Files, Charlotte, N.C.

87. Ibid.

88. Ibid.

Chapter 4

"Unto The Least Of These"

1922 — 1929

The tall stained glass windows were tilted inward, letting in sporadic puffs of warm air which ruffled the pages of the children's hymnbooks. The fragrance of the flowers next to the altar was caught in the circling breeze, already laden with the pungent aroma of freshly-waxed oak.

The Rev. William Wheeler breathed in the redolence of Easter morning as he looked out over his congregation in St. Mary's Chapel, some barely visible behind the high-backed benches. All the children were there: the boys in crisp, white shirts and thin, black ties; the girls in their finest bonnets. Their just-scrubbed faces reflected the sunlight cascading through the prism of the center altar windows as he spoke a prayer over them: "O Thou great Father of the weak, lay thy hand tenderly on all the little children on earth and bless them . . ."[1]

In his message, Wheeler again explained the significance of the campaign which was about to get underway in their behalf. Although it was by far the most ambitious undertaking of the Episcopal Church in North Carolina since the founding of the Thompson Orphanage, the children understood it only in its simplest, most practical terms:

they would no longer have to share a bed in crowded dormitories, feel the biting chill caused by inadequate heat, or bend over an ancient wash tub to scrub their clothes.

Their eyes gleamed in anticipation of the promises as the Rev. Wheeler read the scripture chosen by Bishop Edwin Penick as the theme for the 1924 building campaign, "Inasmuch as ye have done it unto one of the least of these, my brethren, ye have done it unto me." Row after row, the children, nudged by a nearly imperceptible nod from their cottage matron, filed out behind William Wheeler into the bright sunlight of Easter morning.

In 1922, when William Wheeler rattled on to the Thompson Orphanage campus in his 'tin lizzie,' there were nearly 3,000 orphans in North Carolina, and another 3,000 destitute children also in need of care. During its 36-year history, the Thompson Orphanage had taken in over 600 such children but because of inadequate space, had turned away a great many more. There were 85 children crowded into the orphanage in September, 1922, with more anticipated since fur-

William Wheeler leads Sunday worship in St. Mary's Chapel, 1924.

nishing was complete in the Edwin A. Osborne "Baby Cottage." It was apparent that to care for any more needy children, the Thompson Orphanage would have to expand.

Over the next four years, the sounds of building construction became familiar as childrens' laughter across the campus as the orphanage determined to improve living conditions and increase its capacity. The pounding cadence began between 1922-1923 with construction of the Sadie Tucker Williamson Infirmary.

William Williamson, who gave the funds for the infirmary in memory of his wife, added to the original bequest to cover the total building costs and paid for the equipment in the operating room, diet kitchen, nurses' bedroom and the office. The large dormitory on the first floor of the infirmary was furnished in memory of Lemuel Neely Bingham by his sisters, and the second floor by the church school of the Church of the Holy Comforter, Charlotte. A baby ward was

equipped by the junior hospital guild.

Although it was not completed in time to handle the Spring bout with measles and whooping cough, a threatened epidemic of flue in December, 1923, was cut short by isolating the first cases in the new infirmary. According to Wheeler's annual report for the year ending in 1923, over 30 children were treated in the infirmary during its first month of operation.

The infirmary was an important addition, but much more was needed to improve the physical conditions at Thompson Orphanage. In 1923, the three Bishops of the state appointed a Tri-Diocesan Committee to study the needs of the orphanage and bring recommendations to the Board of Managers. The committee's report, completed in September, 1923 and unanimously approved by the Board of Managers on January 30, 1924, resulted in one of the most ambitious projects ever undertaken by the orphanage: a $150,000 building and improvement program to include three cottages, an administration building, a laundry, central heating plant, and numerous repairs.

THE BUILDING CAMPAIGN

Edwin A. Penick, Bishop Coadjutor of the Diocese of North Carolina, was named executive chairman and Edwin Osborne, honorary chairman of the campaign slated for the week of May 25 to June 1, 1924, with May 25 set aside as "Thompson Orphanage Sunday" across the state. From headquarters in St. Peter's Parish House, Bishop Penick supervised the activities of the general committee made up of ten representatives each from the three dioceses. The general campaign committee was led in each diocese by the Bishop: Rt. Rev. Thomas C. Darst for the Diocese of East Carolina; Rt. Rev. Junius M. Horner for the Diocese of Western Carolina; and Rt. Rev. Joseph B. Cheshire for the Diocese of North Carolina. Quotas were assigned for each diocese: $87,000 — Diocese of North Carolina; $25,000 — Diocese of Western Carolina; $37,500 — Diocese of East Carolina. This was the first time in its history that the orphanage had made a direct appeal for funds slated for a specific purpose.

The professional fund-raising firm of Ward, Wells, Greshman & Gates in New York, was hired in February, 1924 to help direct the campaign which was elaborately organized and had the endorsement of church officials from across the state as well as influential leaders in the Charlotte area. A resolution in support of the campaign was publicly issued by the Charlotte Chamber of Commerce, and Charlotte Mayor, J.O. Walker called the orphanage an asset to the city.

> It gives me great pleasure to tell you how much we love the Thompson Orphanage. Personally I feel that it is a wonderful asset to the City and the work under present and past management has been carried on in a manner that does credit to your Church ... Do not hesitate to call on me for anything that you think I might do for you."[2]

Prominent Charlotte businessman J.B. Ivey called the campaign "a most worthy cause" adding, "every citizen in Charlotte should be interested in it."[3] But perhaps the most meaningful statements of support came from public school officials whose primary contact with Thompson Orphanage was through the behavior of the children:

> ... Repeatedly the statement has been made by some of the teachers that the children from the orphanage were doing much better work than many other children of greater ability. We account for the difference by the time given to study in a definite schedule that I feel sure you maintain ... Let me repeat the statement that we are pleased with the habits of courtesy, fairness, honesty, and industry that you have developed in these little orphans. Elmer H. Garinger, Principal, Central High School.[4]

A.M. Elliott, principal of Alexander Graham Junior High School expressed similar respect for the performance of Thompson Orphanage children in that school: "The knowledge that pupils with every advantage and from the so-called best families are over-shadowed by the pupils from the orphanage in deportment should be a source of great pride to you."[5]

The first step in the campaign was to issue a 12-page "Survey of Needs" booklet, mailed in January, 1924 to the publicity agents in each parish for distribution to every member family. In it were graphically portrayed a dormitory room with two facing rows of iron beds, thin blankets draped neatly over sagging mattresses and the caption "One Of Our Bed Rooms — Two To Each Bed," and the dilapidated laundry with young girls hunched over deep wash basins. Another photo of a room, filled to capacity with children, declared, "Our largest room on a rainy day. Floor Space 30×18. 53 Children, One Window."[6]

On April 29, 1924, the first edition of a small campaign newsletter, *Inasmuch,* made its appearance with an article by the Rev. William Wheeler plainly stating the problems of "poor and meagre equipment" and overcrowded conditions which made a "normal home life" at the Thompson Orphanage nearly impossible. Of the 108 children in the orphanage in 1924, fifty-three lived in old Thompson Hall and 16 slept in one room, two each in a single bed. "You cannot build good children," declared the superintendent, "in such an environment."[7]

Bishop Edwin Penick was an enthusiastic

From a "Survey of Needs," back-breaking work in the old laundry.

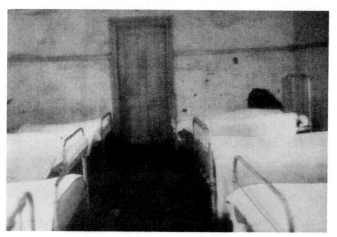

Thompson Hall dormitory, two to a bed.

and prolific coordinator for the campaign, producing a variety of materials designed to tug at the hearts and purse strings of the state's church members. In the second edition of *Inasmuch,* he explained:

The friends of Thompson Orphanage have realized for many years the need for new buildings and improved equipment at the Orphanage. As long ago as 1911, an article in the 'Carolina Churchman' described the equipment as follows: "At each meeting the necessity for new buildings becomes more apparent. Each year the old walls are a little more cracked, the old floors more worn and the general conditions of the place worse. No one who visits the present edifice fails to realize how urgent is the necessity for new and sanitary buildings and equipment. Will the Church people of North Carolina build an Orphanage that will be a credit and not a reproach to the name of the Church we love?" I beg leave to call the attention of the

church to the fact that all of the equipment referred to in this manner in 1911, is still in use at our Orphanage and the passing of thirteen years has not improved the picture.[8]

In a list of facts to be used by campaign speakers, Bishop Penick minced few words.

Last Thanksgiving one Presbyterian Church in N.C. gave a larger offering to the Presbyterian Orphanage than the 278 Parishes and missions of N.C. gave to the Thompson Orphanage in their Thanksgiving collection. Our people do not love little children less, — they just do not understand the need ... If each member of our Church could visit the Orphanage and have a little hand put into his in trusting search of the love for which a small heart is hungering, there would need be no Campaign. Their goodness and their affection make the heart and the pocketbook overflow.[9]

He also created an "Orphanage Catechism" proffering questions about the institution and providing the appropriate responses. The "Catechism" promised, "He who gives a child a home builds palaces in Kingdom Come."[10]

On Sunday, May 18, 1924, when the "Orphanage Catechism" was read in the churches, a letter was also directed to the children of the Sunday Schools from Robert B. Owens, chairman of the Sunday School Committee, describing the orphanage as "a big boy who has outgrown his suit."

Now, we have in Charlotte a big boy who has outgrown his suit, and worse than that, it is almost worn out besides — in fact parts of it have been patched so many times that it is hard to tell which is suit and which is patches. You have never seen him, perhaps, but he is a boy that you are very much interested in, for you have been hearing about him, and sending him things ... Would you like to know his name? Very well, I will tell you. His name is "THOMPSON ORPHANAGE!" ... He needs a new suit, and I want you to help to get it for him.[11]

In an address to campaign workers in Charlotte on the eve of Orphanage Sunday, the Rev. George Floyd Rogers, rector of St. Peter's Church and a member of the campaign executive committee insisted, "We as God-fearing Christ-living and child-serving people must make this campaign a success."[12] And they did.

Episcopalians from across the state responded with 3,500 pledges for a total of $179,191.51 as reported by campaign treasurer, the Rev. John Long Jackson, on July 25, 1924. Many public-spirited citizens of Charlotte also contributed to the campaign in support of the orphanage operating in their city.

Two gifts of $21,000 each made up the bulk of the East Carolina contributions, since the diocese had also committeed to work for the Japanese Reconstruction during May. Christ Church in Raleigh contributed $21,000 to construct a girls' dormitory cottage, and Mrs. Ashby L. Baker, a member of Christ Church, gave $21,000 for a boys' cottage. Among the gifts listed for the North Carolina Diocese was $149.49 from the Chapel of St. Mary the Virgin, whose only congregation was the children and staff of the Thompson Orphanage.[13]

GETTING UNDERWAY

During the summer of 1924, the Board of Managers settled a long-running discussion which had a significant impact on the building program, instructing the Executive Committee to proceed with development of the orphanage on its present site. Only the Rev. George Floyd Rogers, chairman of the finance committee, disagreed, tactfully expressing his eagerness to cooperate in the development of the institution wherever it was located, but entering for the record, his opinion that it was not in "the best interest of the institution to continue the development of the present site."[14]

The contract for designing and supervising construction of the first two cottages in the building program was awarded August 4, 1924 to architect M.R. Marsh. At its September 8, 1924 meeting, the Executive Committee set out a proposed order of building construction, beginning with the central heating plant and laundry followed by two cottages housing 24 children each, laundry machinery, administration building, a third cottage to replace old Bronson Hall, the two East Carolina cottages and other needed improvements which included beautification and landscaping of the grounds, fencing the farm land, and building an attractive entrance gate. Construction was estimated to extend into 1926.

Directing these activities were members of the building committee: F.W. Glover, chairman, Dr. W. Myers Hunter, orphanage physician, Miss Emma Hall, R.H. Bouligny, and landscape architect Earl S. Draper who had come to Charlotte from Massachusetts to help design the distinctive, tree-lined avenues of the Myers Park suburb.

'FAITHFUL AND PERSEVERING' SERVANT DIES

The excitement generated by the successful fund-raising campaign was dampened in August, 1924 by the death of the institution's second superintendent, the Rev. Walter J. Smith. It was noted by the Board of Managers at the time of his death that for 24 years, "without intermission he rendered good, faithful and self-denying service."

> Though of a delicate constitution, he was always faithful and persevering in the discharge of the onerous and responsible duties of position as temporal and spiritual father of the children, and as superintendent and business manager of the Orphanage, and in the performance of every trust reposed in him. He was untiring and painstaking in his labors and with an eye single to the moral, temporal, and spiritual welfare of the children under his care . . . and in spite of many disadvantages, with limited means, he brought up a number of well trained young men and women who will carry the impression of the Church and his fatherly care upon their lives and characters wherever they may go.[15]

The memorial tribute was written by Edwin Osborne.

In January, 1925 the children, staff, and members of the Board presented a brass altar cross to St. Mary's Chapel in memory of Walter Smith, and in March, 1928, the Federation Cottage was permanently re-named Smith Cottage in his honor.

PROMISES BECOME REALITY

Sounds of building activity echoed across campus beginning in 1925, physical evidence of the promised new orphanage. With obvious pride, William Wheeler began his annual report covering the year 1925: "Because of the wonderful generosity of the supporters of the Thompson Orphanage . . . all the children entrusted to our care are now housed in new and beautiful modern brick cottages, which are safe, sanitary, wonderfully heated by the fine new central heating plant, well lighted and ventilated and splendidly equipped."

The first to be completed was Baker Cottage for boys, built in memory of Ashby Lee Baker by his wife Minnie Tucker, and sons Ashby Lee, Jr. and Julian Tucker Baker. It stood next to Stedman Cottage and at the opposite end of campus from the Williamson Infirmary, named for Mrs. Baker's sister.

A cottage of similar design for girls was built between the Baker and Osborne cottages at a cost of $19,339 plus $2,000 in furnishings. It was called Christ Church Cottage since funds were given by the St. Agnes Guild and other members of Christ Church in Raleigh.

At the edge of campus, beyond the infirmary, Kenan Cottage for girls also opened in 1925, a gift of Mrs. Graham Kenan of the Diocese of East Carolina. Built in memory of Lily Kenan Flagler, the cottage was occasionally referred to as the Flagler building, and sometimes as the East Carolina cottage. It was first used to house the children who had lived in the old wooden building known as Bronson Hall.

In his report to the Board in 1925, Wheeler quoted from an article in the *Raleigh News and Observer* by a member of the State Board of Public Welfare which said, "I have never seen anything more attractive and homelike than the Thompson Orphanage at Charlotte. The whole Episcopal Church is to be congratulated."[16]

In August, 1925 the new laundry opened, built with donations from St. Paul's Church in Winston-Salem, and, as the superintendent observed, "has been turning our splendid work every week since. The older boys and girls learned very quickly how to operate the machines and have been doing work every bit as fine as that of the best professional laundries."[17] The building cost $9,000 to construct, and $7,613.30 to equip.

Adjacent to the laundry was the welcomed new heating plant, "making every building warm and cozy for the first time in the nearly 40 years' existence of the institution."[18]

A concrete driveway and sidewalks to each building replaced the dirt and gravel paths, and enabled the children to use their roller skates. Landscape architect Earl Draper donated the design and materials for beautifying the grounds at no charge, a plan which included setting out 25 willow oak trees in January, 1926.

Several new buildings were added to the farm, including a concrete silo, and a portion of the land enclosed "with a strong wire fence."[19] The floor in the chapel was repaired, and the Stedman and Federation cottages painted.

NEW EXPENSES

The flurry of building activity brought with it not only additional space, but additional expense. New staff members were needed, including a nurse for the infirmary, a nurse/dietician for the baby cottage, additional matrons and substitute matrons, a laundry supervisor, a supervisor for the heating plant and a recreational director. Heating and maintenance costs increased too. In the face of its most expensive year to date, the orphanage began 1925 with only $4,400 in the bank and a prospective budget of $36,000. To help alleviate the financial pinch and heavy reliance on the Thanksgiving Offering, the Board authorized that the Sunday nearest the May 6 birthday of Edwin Osborne be observed in every parish and mission as "Osborne Thanksgiving Day," with all contributions going directly to the orphanage. The Board also suggested that groups or individuals could take on the cost of caring for one child at $300 a year, or annually clothing that child for $75.

A special financial committee was named to direct the Osborne Thanksgiving Day appeal: F.W. Glover, Lewis Burwell, A.L. Bovie and R.H. Bouligny. Another issue of the magazine *Inasmuch* was mailed out along with special envelopes for the May 3, 1925 collection which added over $3,000 to orphanage operating funds.

By the end of April, 1926, plans by architect M.R. Marsh were approved for the new administration building, to be built on the site of the old farmer's cottage, at a cost of approximately $42,000. Set in the center of the campus between Osborne Cottage and Federation Cottage, now called Smith Cottage in memory of the second superintendent, the new building was completed in September, 1926 and dedicated in May, 1927 to the memory of Benjamin Swan Bronson.

In addition to offices, the building contained a library, kindergarten, and gymnasium "convertible into an assembly hall and . . . equipped with a handsome curtain and back drops and also with portable footlights, dressing rooms and piano."[20] The facilities were often used by local churches, nearby Central High School, and others for team practices, games and rehearsals. In June, 1929 the gym was turned into a makeshift hotel to help house some of the over 25,000 people who attended the 39th Reunion of Confederate Veterans in Charlotte.[21]

In the annual Thanksgiving Appeal letter for 1926, ghostwritten in all likelihood by the superintendent, the children of Thompson Orphanage expressed their gratitude for the many additions to the campus: the infirmary ("We are healthy . . . If you are not, please come to our Infirmary, and our good friends, the doctors, will take out your tonsils . . . and then you will be as fat and happy as we are."); the central heating plant ("We are warm . . . All we have to do is to turn on the radiator which sizzles a little, and then, there your are — warm as toast."); the laundry ("We are clean . . . Our clothes washing is fun now."); the new cottages ("Lots of sunlight and fresh air and new beds and lockers for each of us.").[22] However, the children pointed out in their letter, "We are expensive. The fine new buildings that you have put up . . . will cost a lot of money to keep up. Our family is very large, 112 in all. This means that we cost more to feed because more of us are eating, and our appetites are all right."[23]

A PERFECT MAN

Just a month after the new administration building was finished, the man whose singular heart's desire was to see the progress of Thompson Orphanage, died quietly at his home on West Eleventh Street. Edwin A. Osborne was 89 when he died on October 12, 1926. He was eulogized by members of the Executive Committee as "a lover of men, a friend of the helpless, and especially a fatherly minister to the fatherless little children, who filled a long life of active benevolence with sagacity, affection and unweariness in well-doing whose name will be remembered throughout all generations and his good deeds be perpetuated in the characters of those he built up in the nurture and admonition of the Lord." At his funeral, held the following day at St. Peter's Church, Bishop Joseph B. Cheshire remarked without hesitation, "He was the best man I ever knew."[24]

Though beloved by all during his 29 years of devotion to Thompson Orphanage, Osborne may have received the most fitting tribute of all from the children.

> "A matron one night was reproving some of her boys for being a little too boisterous, whereupon one of them said, 'You don't want us to be perfect, do you?' The matron replied, 'No, of course not. Only one person is perfect, and by the way, who is that?' Immediately a chorus of boys' voices shouted out, 'Mr. Osborne.'!"[25]

This story was reported in the February, 1927 edition of *The Carolina Churchman*.

In October, 1928, the Executive Committee decided that instead of building a new chapel, major repairs should be made to the existing St. Mary's, using money from the undesignated balance of the building fund.

> These repairs included new windows and floors, new choir stalls and altar rail, a handsome reredos, and an artistic porch at the front entrance. These repairs were carried out under the direction of the Rev. Robert Bruce Owens, rector of the Church of the Holy Comforter, Charlotte, who submitted the beautiful designs and did some of the exquisite carving himself.[26]

NO GAS STATIONS OR GOLF COURSES

Like all those connected with Thompson Orphanage, members of the Executive Committee took great pride in the new, modern look of the campus and sought to preserve it, apparently agreeing with the estimation of recreation director David Yates in 1926, "that without an inviting and pleasing landscape setting for its buildings, an institution cannot reach its highest efficiency."[27] Executive Committee members rejected a request by a prominent local businessman to lease a portion of the East Fourth Street frontage in 1926 for a gas station, and, after heated debate, turned down a proposal in

A special mailing piece shows a panoramic view

September, 1929, to convert the rear of the property to a golf course, the major opposition being the unthinkable possibility of the course being open on Sunday. Minutes from Executive Committee meetings during this time affirm, "the question of Sunday golf evoked considerable discussion" with the Rev. Robert Bruce Owens submitting a hypothetical motion that "if the rear of the property be rented for golf purposes, the playing of golf on Sunday be not allowed."[28] The golfers were finally abandoned in favor of "a sufficient number of cattle . . . to keep down the grass and weeds in the pasture."[29] Executive Committee members did, however, allow friendly condemnation of a 12-foot right-of-way in September, 1927 so that Southern Power Company could erect a steel tower "absolutely necessary for conveying power for the use of the city."[30]

CHILDREN VENTURE INTO COMMUNITY LIFE

The years between 1922 and 1929, though preoccupied with material emendation within the boundaries of the campus, were significant, primarily for the children, as a period of melding more effectively into the Charlotte community. They attended public schools and joined school teams, participated in scouting, went to local Episcopal churches, and generally became more aware of community and denominational responsibilities.

Their assimilation into the public school system came in stages. Some had been attending since 1916, then in 1923 all children above sixth grade were enrolled. In 1924 orphanage children above third grade went to public schools and finally, in 1926, all school-aged children left their small but familiar classrooms in the campus school to enter the mainstream of public education. In Charlotte's schools they received five hours of daily instruction instead of the three and one-half hours in the campus school. Only a kindergarten remained on the campus, taught in Bronson Hall by Miss Elsie Nall and "universally conceded to be a 'model' school room,"[31] placing the orphanage in the unique position of having to refuse requests from Charlotte parents who wanted to enroll their children.

The value of the social experience provided by public education was praised by David W. Yates, recreational director and office secretary at the orphanage:

> Since they began to attend the city schools, the children's lives have been greatly broadened and enriched by the new interests and friendships which they have acquired. They are beginning to have the same attitude toward life as other boys and girls

of Thompson Orphanage as it appeared in 1927.

The children needed many more clothes when they began attending school off campus. The St. Peters's Church Service League responded by providing most of the childrens' clothes and necessary school equipment. During 1927 a Clothing Committee was organized by John Long Jackson, rector of St. Martin's Church in Charlotte, in an effort to make individuals and organizations responsible for a child's annual clothing needs. Eighty-nine of the 111 children in the orphanage in 1928 received their clothing through the work of this committee. Some groups donated clothes and others gave money to purchase new items such as shoes, hats, and coats. Sewing and mending tasks were taken over by the Thompson Orphanage Aid Committee, a group of women representing the three Charlotte parishes who met each Thursday morning to work in the orphanage sewing room.

Spiritual training was considered as important for the growing orphanage children as academic preparation, each day beginning with 8 o'clock services in St. Mary's Chapel in addition to prayers and Bible reading in the cottages. The older boys were trained to lead services for special occasions such as during Lent. Sunday School and morning worship were held on campus until 1926 when the older children were en-

rolled in Sunday School classes at St. Peter's Church, and later at St. Martin's. A Young People's Service League, organized in 1923, met on Sunday afternoons in St. Mary's Chapel. Its members, all children of the orphanage, were remarkably attuned to the needs of others, supporting church relief programs for the Near East and Japan, giving to the Red Cross, and contributing toward the tuition for a partially blind fellow resident to attend Lees-McRae Institute. At Christmas they delivered stockings, fruit, and toys to children in the surrounding Brooklyn and Cherry neighborhoods, and in 1926 were recognized by *The Charlotte Observer* for their support of flood disaster relief in Florida:

> Possibly the largest single contribution yet received by The Observer for the Florida storm relief fund came yesterday — not the largest in dollars and cents, but the largest perhaps in what it represents. It was a contribution of $3.98 made by the children in the Thompson Orphanage at Charlotte . . . It is not unlikely that some of them gave all the money they had because their tender little hearts were drawn out in sympathy for the suffering and destitute in the storm stricken area. 'Of such is the kingdom of heaven.'[33]

The money they put in the offering plates and mite box was their own, a portion of small wages paid for their campus chores. The orphanage dairy herd, up to 20 Holstein and Guernsey cows in 1926, kept the older boys busy while the girls did laundry and housework, allowing them to learn "the things necessary in building and maintaining a home."[34] Since there was no central dining room, the children in each cottage shared responsibility for preparing and serving meals, stacking, washing, and drying dishes used for 24 or more people each meal, and afterwards, sweeping the wooden floors to a sheen with a stiff broom and mop.

VALUE IN PLAY

Organized recreation, too, was becoming an increasingly important aspect of the childrens' daily routine, aiding greatly their interraction with other children in the community. In his annual report for 1924, the superintendent affirmed, "Play is now recognized as essential in the development of character. Dr. Luther H. Gullicke says, 'If you want to know what a child is, study his play; if you want to affect what he shall be, direct his play.' "[35]

Miss Ellen Lay was the first recreational director in 1923. Under her direction "the children enjoyed a number of field meets and tournaments, two athletic teams were organized and the tennis court was built."[36] David Yates assumed the position of recreational director in 1924, organizing a variety of teams including one for football, enrolling the children in the YMCA and YWCA, forming a Boy Scout troop and Girl Reserve Club on campus, and promoting special trips for the children. Many of them saw the ocean for the first time on a trip to Wrightsville Beach during the summer of 1924, romping through the surf in bathing suits donated by local citizens through an appeal in Charlotte newspapers. Yates described life on campus as "a combination of work, study, play, and worship" and was convinced that, "One of the main reasons why the children are so healthy is that most of their time outside of school is spent in playing on the campus."[37] Favorite activities were baseball, tennis, basketball, football and roller skating. One of the first activities in the new gym was the New Year's Eve, 1926, basketball game in which the children soundly defeated a team of orphanage alumni.

Charles Milstead succeeded David Yates in 1927, supported in his efforts by a new recrea-

Tennis was a popular sport. Smith Cottage is in the background.

tion committee consisting of orphanage physician Dr. Myers Hunter as chairman, W.J. Cartier, superintendent of the city's playgrounds, Otto Gullickson, recreation director for the city schools, and Mrs. Sam Maxwell. The orphanage playground became linked to the city's recreation system in 1929, the children specifying, "Please call us 'Thompson Park,' and not 'Thompson Orphanage.' "[38]

CONTINUING CHALLENGES

The means of administering and supervising the ever-widening scope of orphanage life, and keeping up with developing trends in institutional child care became two of the greatest challenges of the period between 1925 and 1929. With the increased enrollment brought about by completion of the new cottages, William Wheeler recognized the need to more thoroughly investigate each child's circumstances before admission. "Several children have been turned over to relatives and friends," he reported to the Board of Managers in 1925, "after investigations which disclosed the existence of relatives who, since the placing of the children, had become able to care for them."[39] He proposed that the orphanage hire a full-time case worker who could help secure more financial support from living relatives or from organizations, and identify children who might be better served elsewhere. There was not enough money in the budget, however, to support such a case-worker.

The institution also found itself at odds with a growing national trend which sought to stamp orphanages as obsolete. The argument was precipitated by the declining number of true orphans, and a general feeling against prolonged residential care. During the 1920's, a survey by the Children's Bureau of the United States Department of Labor revealed that of 19,879 dependent children in nine states, 5 per cent were full orphans, 30 per cent half-orphans, and 65 per cent had both parents living.[40] Questions about the appropriateness of institutional care for these children were raised in professional conferences across the nation, and North Carolina's orphanages, too, struggled with decisions concerning admission.

There were so many applications for admission to the Thompson Orphanage that the Board of Managers in January, 1927, was compelled to limit total enrollment to 112 children, very few of whom were full orphans. Of the 121 children cared for during 1927, 26 were full orphans, 70 were half-orphans, and 25 had both parents living. William Wheeler defended the institution's acceptance of dependent children who had living parents, explaining to the Board of Managers in January, 1928:

> It is comparatively easy to care for the full orphan and it is becoming easier to care for the half orphan, especially the fatherless, through 'Mother's Aid,' but the hardest relief to secure is that for the child that has both parents living; one parent may be insane, or committed to jail for a long term, and the other parent may be a helpless invalid, or immoral, or merely incompetent, but many institutes absolutely refuse to give aid to the unfortunate child of such parents, who are usually in deeper need and distress, than those children that are orphans or semi-orphans.[41]

Wheeler kept constantly abreast of developments in the field of child welfare, particularly through involvement in the North Carolina Orphan Association which he headed in 1927. It was through the Association that an annual Thanksgiving Day campaign was promoted throughout the state which asked each citizen to give a day's income to the dependent children of North Carolina. Proceeds from the campaign were divided among member institutions, including Thompson Orphanage. Addressing the Association in 1928, North Carolina Governor Angus W. McLean praised the work of the state's approximately 25 orphanages, expressing his opinion that government should not enter the field of orphan protection "since the work is now being so well cared for by the various fraternal and religious organizations."[42] The governor did suggest that the state's welfare workers "might render assistance in promoting the work of the orphanges."[43] Welfare workers had begun to provide for children who did not need to be placed in orphanages by boarding them in foster homes.

William Wheeler had his own ideas about how to relieve the burden on the state's orphanages: " . . . an expert diagnosis of each case is the means of relieving all the present and future congestion in Institutions."[44] Over the years, it had become relatively easy to get children placed in an orphanage, the only real requirement being the availability of space. Seldom was there adequate case study to determine if placement in an orphanage was the most appropriate means of care. The first records of children placed at Thompson Orphanage were sketchy notations in Edwin Osborne's *Superintendent's Record,* but there were no standard forms for admission or discharge until 1903, and no required physical or mental exams until late in 1920.

For some children, whether orphaned or not, long-term residence in an institution was called for, but, agreed the superintendent, "one medicine for every child is no longer the rule . . . "[45] William Wheeler still believed in the importance of residential orphanage care, especially in developing and molding childrens' character. "I think we are all apt to forget in this age of machine made products and mass movements," he told the Board in his 1929 annual report, "that character is still hand made and heart made."[46]

But the shaping of 'hand made' character was expensive and the job of finding the money to support the work of the orphanage continued to be a difficult one. The Board of Managers tried various plans, including assessing each diocese according to the numbers of children in residence and appointing an agent to encourage the parishes to meet their share of the maintenance costs. The institution was established to care for orphan and destitute children regardless of church affiliation, and, on the average, only 40 per cent of the children each year came from Episcopal backgrounds. The Duke Endowment, established in December, 1924, appropriated a certain amount each year to the Thompson Orphanage, based on the numbers of children receiving care, and some parents or other relatives of children in the institution contributed regularly to their support. Still, budget cuts and borrowing were commonplace.

The institution had to do some quick shuffling in December, 1927 to provide adequate leadership when a sudden serious illness forced William Wheeler out of the superintendent's job until March 1, 1928. During the interim, John Long Jackson, rector of St. Martin's Church, took over administrative duties and John Moore Walker, rector of St. Peter's Church, assumed the pastoral responsibilities. Wheeler's illness brought into focus the need for an assistant superintendent or business manager, to ensure continuity in the operation of the orphanage and maintenance of financial support. Budget restraints notwithstanding, A.S. Bynum was hired in July, 1929 as the first assistant superintendent, at a salary of $150 a month plus a house and garden plot and the privilege of buying food and fuel at wholesale rates.[47]

In 1929, the institution also considered changing its name to better reflect a changing role. A committee consisting of the Rev. Joseph Cheshire, the Rev. Samuel B. Stroup, and Dr. William Cobb Whitfield was appointed in March, 1929 to study the idea and in June the Board of Managers voted unanimously to become the "Thompson Episcopal Home."[48] At their next meeting, in January, 1930, members of the Board rescinded the proposal on the advice of attorney Hamilton C. Jones who said the institution could only use the legal name as set forth in the original deed.[49]

FINANCES AND FAITH

In his annual report covering the year 1929, William Wheeler summarized the financial outlook of the orphanage as a correlation between finances and faith.

> The past year was fraught with considerable financial strain and worry . . . As far back as the March meeting of the Executive Committee, the condition of the Current Fund was such as to call forth a resolution authorizing the treasurer to borrow money to meet salaries and outstanding obligations. Again, in the Fall of the year, a similar resolution was passed, and yet, due largely to the work of the Finance Committee, decreasing expenditures and reducing the staff, the treasurer was enabled to end the year without borrowing one penny, and with all bills paid. Surely this ought to be not only a cause for satisfaction but also a stimulus to our Faith. We have under consideration at this meeting the budget and the financial needs for the coming year. Let us be thoughtful not to omit the most important item of Faith, and while seeking first the kingdom of God for His little ones, believe that all necessary financial help will be forthcoming.[50]

In the face of the inevitable and deepening national Depression, the exercise of faith would become an essential feature of daily life at the Thompson Orphanage. Foreseeing harder years ahead, William Wheeler closed his report in January, 1930, with a preparatory challenge:

> Since we have set up high standards of care for the children committed to us, let us have Faith to go forward and continue to progress. If we are going to do the work at all, let us do it with strict adherence to the most approved methods of child care, never forgetting that understanding, sympathy, insight and love, are much more valuable and effective in producing lasting results for good, than mere arbitrary and mechanical programs . . . May God give us wisdom both to perceive and know what things we ought to do and also grace and power FAITHFULLY to fulfill the same.[51]

FOOTNOTES

1. *Inasmuch,* No. 4, May, 1924, p. 3, Edwin A. Penick Papers, Thompson Orphanage, 1920-1949, Diocesan House, Raleigh, N.C.

2. "Comments By Citizens of Charlotte Regarding Thompson Orphanage," Edwin A. Penick Papers, Thompson Orphanage, 1920-1949, Diocesan House, Raleigh, N.C.

3. Ibid.

4. Ibid.

5. Ibid.

6. *Survey of Needs* (Charlotte: Observer Printing House, 1924), p. 5.

7. *Inasmuch,* No. 1, April 29, 1924, p. 3, Edwin A. Penick Papers, Thompson Orphanage, 1920-1949, Diocesan House, Raleigh, N.C.

8. *Inasmuch,* No. 2, May 6, 1924, p. 1, Edwin A. Penick Papers, Thompson Orphanage, 1920-1949, Diocesan House, Raleigh, N.C.

9. "Facts For Speakers About Thompson Orphanage," Edwin A. Penick Papers, Thompson Orphanage, 1920-1949, Diocesan House, Raleigh, N.C.

10. "Orphanage Catechism," Edwin A. Penick Papers, Thompson Orphanage, 1920-1949, Diocesan House, Raleigh, N.C.

11. Robert B. Owens to Boys and Girls of the Church School, Edwin A. Penick Papers, Thompson Orphanage, 1920-1949, Diocesan House, Raleigh, N.C.

12. "Episcopalians Gather At Dinner Here Tonight," *The Charlotte Observer,* May 24, 1924, p. 6.

13. "Local Parishes Exceed Quotas," *The Charlotte Observer,* May 29, 1924. p. 2.

14. "Minutes," Executive Committee, June 17, 1924.

15. "Minutes," Executive Committee, September 8, 1924.

16. "Annual Report," January, 1926, p. 1.

17. Ibid.

18. Ibid.

19. Ibid.

20. *The Carolina Churchman,* February, 1927, p. 12.

21. Janette T. Greenwood, *On the Home Front: Charlotte During the Civil War,* ed. Stuart C. Schwartz (Charlotte: Mint Museum, 1982), p. 19.

22. Thanksgiving Appeal Letter, November, 1926, Edwin A. Penick Papers, Thompson Orphanage, 1920-1949, Diocesan House, Raleigh, N.C.

23. Ibid.

24. Mary Anna Turner, "A Fond Recollection," *Saint Peter's Episcopal Church, 1834-1984 — A Fond Remembrance* (n.p.), p. 34.

25. *The Carolina Churchman,* February, 1927, p. 5.

26. Jean Hendrix, "Growth and Progress of Churches in Charlotte," *The Charlotte Observer,* January 21, 1940, sec. 3, p. 9.

27. *The Carolina Churchman,* February, 1927, p. 5.

28. "Minutes," Executive Committee, April 17 and May 2, 1929.

29. "Minutes," Executive Committee, September 6, 1929.

30. "Minutes," Executive Committee, September 6, 1927.

31. *The Carolina Churchman,* February, 1927, p. 12.

32. *The Carolina Churchman,* February, 1925, p. 13.

33. "Orphans Give Their Pennies, Dimes And Nickels to Relief of Florida," undated newspaper clipping, Thompson Orphanage Historical Files, Charlotte, N.C.

34. Hazel Mizelle, "Where Orphaned Children Get Loving Care," *The Charlotte Observer,* May 6, 1928, p. 5.

35. "Annual Report," January, 1925, p. 3.

36. Ibid., p. 2.

37. *The Carolina Churchman,* February, 1925, p. 13.

38. "Annual Report," January, 1929, p. 1.

39. "Annual Report," January, 1925, p. 2.

40. Fink, p. 341.

41. "Annual Report," January 1928, p. 2.

42. "Governor M'Lean Commends Work Of State Orphanages," undated newspaper clipping from *The Raleigh Times,* circa 1928, Thompson Orphanage Historical Files, Charlotte, N.C.

43. Ibid.

44. "Annual Report," January, 1929, p. 3.

45. Ibid.

46. Ibid., p. 4.

47. "Minutes," Executive Committee, July 10, 1929.

48. "Minutes," Board of Managers, June 30, 1929.

49. "Minutes," Board of Managers, January 29, 1930.

50. "Annual Report," January, 1930, p. 3.

51. Ibid.

Chapter 5

Those Hard Years

1929 — 1940

She'd heard there was work at the Thompson Orphanage, and with a baby of her own to provide for, she was determined to get the job.

Her merry black eyes were fixed on the precarious swinging bridge which would take her across Sugar Creek to the neat semi-circle of cottages at the crest of the hill. Though a slight creature, 17-year old Lillie Mae Hart was no stranger to hard work, as testified by her hands which, even in the dim morning light shone like polished mahogany, rubbed smooth by constant toil. She had been able to take care of herself so far, quitting school after the sixth grade to work as a cook for a boarding house in the Billingsville community and learning to cook by doing, studiously reading cookbooks and clipping recipes from newspapers. And it was these skills she carried with her this morning in 1929 to the front door of Baker Cottage.

Mrs. Carpenter peered over the threshold to get a better look at the young black girl, obviously not much older than most of the boys who lived in the cottage. Scrutinizing her up and down, the matron finally shook her head. "I don't know if you can handle it or not," she said, pulling air through her teeth in a sharp whistle, "but we'll

give it a try." Lillie Mae tried, unsuccessfully, to smother a relieved grin as she listened attentively to Mrs. Carpenter explain details about the job which included working in the laundry and cooking for the nearly 24 boys who lived in Baker Cottage. "Yes," she answered Mrs. Carpenter's inquiry, "Yes, a dollar a day is fine."

Following Mrs. Carpenter into the roomy kitchen, Lillie Mae glanced about eagerly, noting the huge coal stove and long, very well worn, wooden table. One of the boys, already late for school, scurried through the room with barely a nod and a hastily formed "Ma'am,' as the door banged shut behind him. "I'm gonna' like it here," thought Lillie Mae to herself. "I'm gonna' like it just fine."

When Herbert Hoover was elected President in November, 1928, he promised, "We in America today are nearer to the final triumph over poverty than ever before in the history of any land."[1] Less than a year later the entire country was thrown into a desperate battle against poverty and economic ruin precipitated by the sudden and decisive crash of the stock market on that Black Thursday in October, 1929; a battle continuing through ruinous years of bank failures, bread lines, and despair known as The Great Depression.

They were years of agony, of "walking everywhere . . . because there was either no gas or no car; swapping eggs for absolute necessities at a penny apiece; working (when any work was available) at five cents an hour, and getting paid in anything but money."[2] Self-respect was a frequent casualty: "That was one time, and I've been through the Reconstruction of the Slave War, that a man simply couldn't make a nickel. It was the worst time I've ever seen or anybody else has that I know of for tryin' to make a dollar."[3] And when families couldn't make it, they turned anywhere they could for help, including orphanages.

NO VACANCY

At Thompson Orphanage, the 'hard years' of the Depression were characterized by reports of "many applications but no vacancies,"[4] of borrowing and budget-slashing, wrestling with over-used buildings that refused to stay repaired, and by a genuine desire to streamline the institution and adhere to developing standards of practice within the field of child welfare.

In the decade between 1929 and 1939, Thompson Orphanage operated at the maximum of its enrollment limit, and on occasion set aside beds in the Infirmary for children in "emergency" situations. But the waiting list rarely shortened, nor did the orphanage's list of needs. To help increase contributions to the annual Thanksgiving Offering which supported operations at the orphanage, the Executive Committee named a special publicity committee in 1930 to coordinate a group of speakers, assigned to give a four-minute speech in each church prior to the collection. The speeches reiterated:

> Unless sufficient funds are obtained to operate the Orphanage at its present high standard, we will have to reduce the number of our worthy children or close one of our several cottages . . . There are 107 children in the Orphanage at the present time. They are all boys and girls for whom the Church is caring and who are in every way deserving . . . Can

we afford to dismiss any of these children to whom we owe such a great responsibility?[5] Speakers were instructed to preface their talk "with a word of grateful appreciation for the loyal backing and support given the Orphanage throughout these past years of hard times."[6]

While raising awareness among church members who gave as liberally as possible to support their orphanage, the publicity campaign could not raise dollars where there were none. The economic times were difficult for everyone in the state and the competition for what relief there was made appeals for aid both touching and numerous. Many of the families who turned to the orphanage for relief found that it, too, suffered the symptoms of want during the Depression. In March, 1932, the chairman of the admissions committee for Thompson Orphanage declared, "while a great many applications had been received, it was unwise in his judgement because of the state of the finances, to take in any more children at this time."[7] By January, 1934, the institution faced $4,000 in unpaid bills, calling on the dioceses to quickly send in contributions still outstanding from the Thanksgiving Offering.

'BUDDY CAN YOU SPARE A DIME?

Thompson Orphanage officials kept one eye on the budget, the other on the doors of the bank. Between 1929 and 1933 there were 215 bank failures in North Carolina, including 3 in Charlotte. On December 8, 1930 a special meeting of the Executive Committee was called after the closing of the First National Bank of Charlotte. The current fund and several special funds, which had been deposited in that bank, were ordered transferred to the near-by Trade Street branch of Independence Trust Company, which, following the 'banking holiday' in 1933, never reopened its doors. But with shrewd financial acumen provided by endowment treasurer Francis O. Clarkson, and Fred W. Glover, head of the finance committee, orphanage funds stayed secure. The endowment maintained a steady growth, even during the Depression, providing the only stable element in the institution's economy. Bank loans were frequently authorized to squeeze the orphanage through tight times, particularly in the Fall as money from the previous year's Thanksgiving Offering ran out. Creditors and members of the staff appeared to have been patient even when bills and paychecks fell long overdue. In 1932, all salaries were cut, and as reported in the minutes of the Executive Committee a "vote of thanks" was directed to staff members "for the fine spirit displayed in the acceptance of the salary cut."[8] Given the staggering rate of unemployment in North Carolina, with one-sixth of all workers on relief,[9] orphanage staff members had little choice. Those few new staff members hired during the period were often expected to fill several functions, such as Janet Mays who came in October, 1931 to work in the laundry, the library, and do some casework.[10]

Numerous schemes were considered, some undertaken, to help trim costs and stretch the budget. Local school children, who in the past had collected and donated fruit and fresh food to the orphanage at Thanksgiving were asked instead to give canned goods, so that some of Thanksgiving could be preserved into later months. Children in Episcopal Sunday Schools across the state donated their used school books to orphanage students. The assistant superintendent managed to secure substantial discounts on coal and freight charges, and the superintendent absorbed various operating expenses in his own salary.

> . . . the items of automobile expense $100, telephone $27, water $30 and gas $100, formerly paid from Current Fund, had been removed from the budget and added to the salary of the Superintendent.[11]

Rental fees for use of the orphanage auditorium by Charlotte's Little Theater were raised from $30 to $50 in January, 1932.

In January, 1933 a campaign was inaugurated through the Young Peoples' Service League in the Diocese of North Carolina to save 'Octagon Soap' wrappers which could be redeemed by the orphanage for cash.[12] Other ideas were rejected, such as the offer "to allow the children of the Orphanage a large selling profit in 'Flurene Nose & Throat Drops.'"[13] The boys were permitted to sell birdhouses which they made in the woodworking shop.

The finance committee asked for, and received, support from the County Commission in July, 1933, to help pay for the care of 19 children from Mecklenburg County in Thompson Orphanage. Commissioners continued their support with an annual appropriation of $600 to the institution.[14]

Wherever a dollar was saved, it seemed, another two were needed to keep up with building repairs and maintenance. Even though many of the buildings had been constructed as late as 1925 or 1926, they got an inordinate amount of use from the average of 100 or more children living at the orphanage on a daily basis. A properties committee was appointed to help keep track of the many needs, and help find ways to meet them.

The first need was to rid all the buildings of termites which, ignoring the quota for campus admissions, had taken up residence in the wooden beams, walls, and floors. The Charlotte Exterminating Company was hired in October, 1932 to eradicate the pests and help guard against their return over the next five years. This unseen danger taken care of, the orphanage then turned its attention to the buildings' more blatant needs. In April, 1933 the exterior of Osborne Cottage and Williamson Infirmary were painted, the ceiling repaired in Osborne Cottage "for the small sum of $75,"[15] and gutters and down spouts replaced on several other buildings. During the next month, the interior of Osborne Cottage got a fresh coat of paint, the matrons pitching in to paint all the beds themselves. The following years were marked by a parade of building repairs and improvements which included replacing the supports for the six columns at the front of the administration building in June, 1934, laying a new sidewalk in September, 1934, with the help of A.S. Bynum and some of the older boys, renovating the heating plant in April, 1935, and making major repairs to Kenan Cottage in October, 1935. In making his report to the monthly meeting of the Executive Committee in November, 1935, the chairman of the building and grounds committee noted "work was progressing in the repairs to the buildings and that, as usual, the carpenters found conditions worse than anticipated."[16]

The stairway in the Baby Cottage was fixed in the Spring of 1938 "to keep the children from walking the banisters."[17] and ceilings were repaired in Smith, Kenan, and the Baby Cottage. The task of keeping up with needed repairs became so overwhelming that assistant superintendent A.S. Bynum was asked by the Executive Committee in June, 1938 to make weekly inspections of all campus buildings.

Thompson Orphanage made its own attempts at relief, besides taking in destitute children, offering its idle farm land to the city for use as gardens for the unemployed. But the social prejudice heightened by the Depression precluded its acceptance, the city manager replying in a letter to the orphanage that, "the land in question would not be profitable due to the surrounding Negro homes."[18]

"HARD TIMES AND CHARITY MEAT"

"Those thirties, they were some hard times,"[19] admitted Baker Cottage cook Lillie Mae (Hart) White, remembering the mornings she rose and walked to work before 5 a.m. to start the fire in the coal stove so the 25 boys who lived in the house could have hot biscuits and syrup for breakfast. Though an excellent cook, her meals during these lean years usually consisted of dried beans, potatoes, cabbage, turnips and soups or stews put together with leftovers. But there was ice cream on Wednesday, and meat, usually chicken, on Sunday. Often the orphanage received what she called "charity meat" from government relief programs which she stretched to last an entire week. She felt sorry for the boys when they complained they couldn't stand another meal of it and slipped them clandestine snacks of peanut butter and jelly sandwiches through the kitchen window. "I guess I spoilt them."[20]

She was what the youngsters in Baker Cottage needed her to be: sister, mother, friend, confidant. She listened to their problems, no mater how trivial they appeared, fussed over their shirt collars, laughed with them and, when the matron was resting, gathered the boys in the kitchen for a rendition of the latest dance steps. Even when they teased, running through the kitchen taunting "Lazy Mae", she knew she also had their respect.

Though she got a vacation each year, Lillie Mae White never took it, preferring instead to work and keep the money. Her attitude typified the determination of the Thompson Orphanage to, as she put it, "make a way out of no way,"[21] during the challenging years of the Depression.

ONE CHILD, MANY MEMORIES

Among those boys who gathered in Lillie Mae's kitchen for unscheduled snacks or a dance lesson was George Powell who came to the orphanage in the year of the stock market crash at age 12. "I was one of the few who was really an orphan,"[22] he remembered, his mother having died when Powell was eight, and his father two years later. After living for a while with an uncle near Tarboro, George Powell and his three brothers, Julian, Bob, and J.D., were sent to the Thompson Orphanage. "You talk about a real feeling of homesickness, it was there," he said. "It took some time to get adjusted. I was first impressed by the number of buildings on the campus and the tremendously large trees and the number of youngsters you would see in one place."[23]

With intense clarity, George Powell recalled memories of life at Thompson Orphanage during the thirties, of rock fighting around the barn, lighting the fire in the basement of the Infirmary to heat hot water, making trips to the ice house, and vying for position when the bread truck made its rounds:

> We had a bread truck that came to the orphanage and we'd all compete to unload the bread because you got a five-cent cake. And then there were those trips to the ice house, from Fourth Street over to Graham. We'd get two or three blocks of ice, chop them up and put them in the ice boxes. We did that two or three times a week in a horse-drawn wagon ... What was left we could sell to the neighbors in Brooklyn and Cherry.[24]

Powell and many of the other boys were friends with Kenneth "Keg" Wheeler, one of the superintendent's four children "who got along best with us orphans."[25] Always part of the crowd, the young Wheeler would join his friends in the cottage for dinner, then run home where his mother would wonder why he wasn't hungry. Like all other children growing up during the era, the boys and girls at Thompson Orphanage made their own amusement, found their own contentment and most often were unaware of daily struggles faced by those responsible for operating and maintaining the institution.

SEEKING DIRECTION

Hoping for a better perspective on the institution's environment and its relationship to the childrens' present and future needs, the Thompson Orphanage, at the request of the superintendent and Executive Committee, invited Miss Claudia Hunter and Dr. Henry W. Crane, member of the faculty of the University of North Carolina and psychiatrist for the State Department of Public Welfare, to visit the campus during November, 1931. They interviewed and observed the staff, tested some of the children, and submitted a lengthy list of recommendations prefaced by Dr. Crane's assurance, "I have never been in any institution for children in which I have felt that there was less of the institutional atmosphere and more of the atmosphere that one finds in the usual family situation,"[26] a fact he attributed to Wheeler's personal attitude toward the children. Miss Hunter agreed:

> Dr. Crane's comment that this was less like an institution than any he was ever in was high commendation of this Superintendent, feeling as he does that almost any home is better for a child than an institution. Lack of firmness and failure to hold children to tasks sometimes, which are essential if children are to be trained, dependable, and morally strong for life outside of the Orphanage later, are traceable, I am sure, to a heart that almost breaks sometimes over these children the Church has intrusted [sic] to him.[27]

During the investigation, the children were given mental and physical tests to help work out a plan to "fit them intelligently for some vocation consonant with their individual traits . . ."[28] At the time there were 109 children at the orphanage, ranging in age from two to nineteen years. The consultants also noted areas of campus social life which needed re-examination, calling for the use of a children's counselor, par-

Story time was a favorite for the children, and superintendent William Wheeler.

ticularly so those who had experienced traumatic events in their past could have someone to talk to, a relaxation of bedtime rules which had all children, regardless of age, retiring between 8:15 p.m. and 8:45 p.m., allowing the older girls to date or entertain friends on campus ("the privilege to depend upon satisfactory home and school work"),[29] and expanding the recreation program which, in economy measures over the preceeding three years, had been severely cut.

The recommendations from the report were acknowledged by the Executive Committee on November 17, 1931, the members pledging to do all they could toward implementing them as quickly as possible. Acceptance of the Charlotte Junior League's offer in March, 1934, to share a caseworker, Thompson Orphanage's share being approximately $300 a year, was an important first step toward more thorough investigation of children's capabilities and circumstances prior to admission. Hours set aside for study hall in the campus library were extended to promote better academic performance in school while those for bedtime were relaxed, allowing the older children to stay up later and providing more opportunities for dating:

> The Superintendent reported two of the older girls had slipped out of their cottage at night and asked for advice in handling the situation. Mr. Balthis moved that a committee . . . consider the plan of allowing the older girls to invite their boy friends from the outside to call upon them.[30]

It was not until 1935 that the orphanage was able to move on the need for organized recreational activities, hiring George Powell, recent orphanage graduate and a physical education major at Appalachian University, as recreation director for the summer. He returned for several summers afterward, as well, to supervise sports and other recreational activities such as "the bag races and foot races" down in the pasture on the Fourth of July.[31] By 1936 the only sign of organized recreation outside the summer program was a boys' basketball team, coached by volunteer James Renwick Wilkes, Jr., and a girls' team coached by two young women from Queens College. The women of the church recognized the need and desired "to be of greater service to the orphanage through the creating of a committee . . . to aid the superintendent and staff in every way possible and chiefly with the social life of the children."[32] A cooperative committee was formed, with members appointed by the chairman of each Auxiliary in the Mecklenburg district, under the direction of Mrs. R.W. Ballard, social service secretary of the Womans' Auxiliary, Diocese of North Carolina.

JUBILEE

Not even the privations of the Depression could keep Thompson Orphanage from observing, and celebrating, its Fiftieth Anniversary in May, 1937. It was an appropriate time, the superintendent pointed out, to profit from the experiences gained over the past years and lay a path for the future. The thrust of any future programs, he told the Board of Managers, should be in

> the making of a more determined effort to provide as efficiently as possible, for each child, an opportunity to develop all those basic needs of human character — good health, cleanliness of body and mind, good moral habits, obedience to proper authority, the best possible education, a knowledge of so-

cial facts, training in good manners, and above all, a knowledge and love of God.[33]

A special Jubilee Committee was appointed at the request of Bishop Edwin A. Penick in October, 1936 to make plans for a celebration to be held May 7, 1937, a date selected as nearest the one hundredth birthday anniversary of the Rev. Edwin A. Osborne. The Rev. Walter Raleigh Noe of the Diocese of East Carolina, was elected chairman of the Jubilee Committee, the Rev. Milton A. Barber, rector emeritus of Christ Church in Raleigh appointed to deliver the historical address, and Mrs. Francis (Josephine) Murdoch of Salisbury assigned to produce a pageant highlighting the history of the orphanage. Among William Wheeler's responsibilities was to foster the growth of an alumni association already functioning in Charlotte and to invite as many former residents of the orphanage as possible to participate in the event. The committee was unanimous in its decision that no offering of any kind, or any financial appeal be made in connection with the celebration.

The achievements of Thompson Orphanage were extolled in various publicity items prepared by Mrs. Maude Waddell, her articles promising, "The story of the Thompson Orphanage is one of romance and deep spiritual beauty and the fulfillment of great vision."[34]

> Saint John's visions might include in a new heaven and a new earth something similar to the glorious Christian achievement to be celebrated on May seventh of the fiftieth year of service of the Thompson Orphanage of Christ's little ones. If the saintly men of God, the Rev. Edwin A. Osborne and the Rev. Benjamin S. Bronson could have known that in but half of one century the minute grain of mustard seed which they sowed in patience, self-denial and faith could flower and blossom as this great humanitarian work has done their joy doubtless would have been complete.[35]

The day of Jubilee dawned with a warm sun to preside over the program set on the orphanage lawn. The first event was the service of Holy Communion at 10 a.m. in St. Mary's Chapel, celebrated by Bishop Edwin Penick with the assistance of Bishop Thomas D. Darst of the Diocese of East Carolina, Bishop Robert E. Gribbin of the Diocese of Western Carolina, and the Rev. William Wheeler. A choir of children from the orphanage, draped in crisp white robes and flouncy bows slightly askew, filled the chapel with their songs. The children were under the direction of William Wall Whidditt, choirmaster and organist at St. Peter's Church, whose dazzling white hair and stately carriage commanded their rapt attention.

After a welcome from Robert Bruce Owens, chairman of the Executive Committee and rector of Charlotte's Church of the Holy Comforter, the Rev. Milton A. Barber delivered his address entitled, "Great Trees from Little Acorns Grow." He boasted, "During the half century of its continuous life, this Orphanage has been the home of about one thousand boys and girls. Some of these went to college; some settled down to good jobs and made their way in the world . . . The Orphanage gave them their start in life and they remember it with affection."[36]

Although there was no formal financial appeal, Dr. Barber emphasized the duty of the state's Episcopal denomination to remain "orphanage conscious."

> In the days of Mr. Osborne and Mr. Smith, the Orphanage had to depend almost entirely on the Orphanage Guilds and the Thanksgiving offerings for its support. Now, the Orphanage is an item in the diocesan budget and a definite amount is furnished for the Orphanage each year . . . Such diocesan recognition of obligations is not only good for the people in the dioceses, educationally and morally. This Orphanage is our very own. Let us recognize our obligation to it in a corporate, as well as in an individual way. And let us stand by our obligation. It takes money to operate an institution like this, but it is money worthily spent . . . In the Act of Incorporation it was stated that 'the object of the said corporation is to prepare orphans and homeless children for the duties and responsibilities of life.' We have tried to be true to that object, which is great, indeed.[37]

He challenged supporters "to go forward in the name of Christ and His church to a greater service to these little ones in the next fifty years."[38]

Francis Osborne Clarkson, grandson of the first superintendent and trustee of the Endowment Fund since 1920, reported next on "A Never Failing Succession of Benefactors" who had contributed gifts, legacies and bequests both

William Wall Whidditt (far right) and the Thompson Orphanage choir at the 1937 Jubilee Celebration.

large and small. The list included $196.75, the fund's first contribution in 1901 from the estate of Mrs. Mary E. Fonville, $44,000 held in trust from Lawrence S. Holt, a bequest of $10,000 from Benjamin N. Duke, and a bequest from "one of the former girls of the Orphanage, Miss Alice Perry" amounting to several hundred dollars.[39] "So far as we know," said Clarkson, "this is the first bequest of this kind to be recorded, and it is typical of the loyalty of the boys and girls who have gone out from the Institution."[40] The total in the Endowment Fund was reported as $161,000.

Bishop Edwin Penick then led prayers of thanks, including one which he wrote and authorized for use in the Diocese of North Carolina:

> Almighty God, who art the father of the fatherless, send Thy blessings upon the Thompson Orphanage, instituted in Thy name. Give patience and wisdom to the officers, teachers and matrons of this home, that they may faithfully discharge the duties committed to their charge. Let the boys and girls grow in grace and earnestness, day by day. Strengthen their bodies, enlighten their minds, purify their hearts and sanctify their wills. Bless all who have contributed to this institution, and raise up, we pray Thee, a never-failing succession of benefactors whose names may be perpetuated through all generations as a blessed memory, and their good deeds accepted; through Jesus Christ our Lord. Amen.[41]

The remainder of the morning's program was filled with 'reminiscences' from some who knew the orphanage best: Mrs. Arabella Smith, widow of the second superintendent; Miss Josephine Osborne, daughter of the first superintendent; Mrs. S. Westray Battle, staunch friend of the institution from the Diocese of Western Carolina; Dr. William Myers Hunter, orphanage physician for over 25 years; Miss Mary Bond Griffin, great-granddaughter of Lewis Thompson; and Tom Myers, a recent orphanage graduate enrolled at the University of North Carolina.

Lunch was a picnic on the grounds, provided by the women of Charlotte's four Episcopal churches and St. Mark's in Long Creek. Tours of the campus were provided while the Central High School band entertained. Throughout the day various participants in the Jubilee celebration were interviewed at the microphones of WSOC radio, set up at a sidewalk desk.

At 2 p.m. Mrs. Josephine Murdoch herded her cast members, including many of the orphanage children and local churchwomen, to the open air stage for the slightly apocryphal but entertaining historical pageant. One scene which must have brought laughter to the audience featured the 'barn brigade,' a group of orphanage boys carrying milking buckets, pitchforks and straw, who dragged across the stage with them one of the dairy cows.

Mrs. Murdoch held a special surprise for last:

> About one thousand boys and girls have gone through this home during the past 50 years. The boy who has had perhaps the highest distinction is E. Jerome Pipes, a clergyman of Rapid City, South Dakota. President Roosevelt, during his Dust Bowl Tour last Summer, visited Rapid City on a Sunday, and attended services at Mr. Pipe's church . . . Today we have the honor and distinction of having a very beautiful message by telegram from Mr. Roosevelt . . . [42]

She then read the message from Franklin D. Roosevelt, President of the United States:

> Please tell the children of the Thompson Orphanage how grateful I am for a remembrance in their prayers. It gives me a great pleasure in connection with the Golden Jubilee of the Orphanage to extend hearty felicitations and warmest personal greetings to the officers who direct this noble work, to the

With a little imagination, this merry-go-round became the "ocean wave."

children who find a home there, and to all who participate in the celebration. My prayer is that God will ever bless and prosper this noble work carried on in behalf of His little ones.[43]

The Jubilee celebration closed with the singing of the national anthem, a familiar hymn, "Jesus, Tender Shepherd, Hear Me," and finally, the children's own song, written by William Wheeler to the tune of "America the Beautiful":

O friends so dear, from far and near,
From Sea to Mountain Crest;
We welcome you with love and cheer,
And offer you our best.
O Thompson Home, dear Thompson Home
Blest Haven built through Love,
A training home for little ones,
Inspired by God above.

On this glad Anniversary
We open wide the door,
To greet you all, with blithesome song
And tales of ancient lore.
O Thompson Home, dear Thompson Home
Blest Haven built through Love;
We sing to thee, all hail to thee,
Entwined with God above.

Our memories are golden too,
So filled with deeds divine;
Of matrons and of teachers true,
Who gave their lives as Thine.
O Thompson Home, dear Thompson Home
May God thy gold refine
And crown each child with nobleness
And every deed divine.

O may the vision that we see
Beyond the passing years,
Come true in all its gloriousness
Undimmed by any tears.
O Thompson Home, dear Thompson Home
God keep thee in His love
And crown thy days with blessedness
Like those of Him above.[44]

MANAGEMENT EXAMINED

In the span between the giddy celebration of 1937 and the end of the decade in 1939, the Thompson Orphanage began formulating plans to mesh the institution more effectively with modern methods of child care and to examine the overall management of the institution with particular emphasis on the skills and training of the staff.

Though the state's overall economy showed marked improvement after 1937, indicating the worst of the Depression had passed, the orphanage Executive Committee continued to take serious note of monthly financial statements, viewing with "apprehension and alarm . . . the steadily mounting deficit . . ."[45] William Wheeler, too, had grown weary of the budgetary morass and increasing pressures of management. Finally, in February, 1939, Bishop Edwin Penick, chairman of the Board of Managers, temporarily relinquished the chair to offer a resolution: "That a special committee be appointed to study the whole matter of the administration of the Orphanage, with the idea of dividing the responsibility of the Superintendent and creating the position of Chaplain."[46] He prefaced the resolution with "appreciation to Mr. Wheeler for his many years of service and his unselfish attitude towards a change in management."[47]

Members of this committee were each Bishop of the Board plus one additional member from each diocese: the Rt. Rev. Thomas C. Darst and the Rev. Walter R. Noe from East Carolina; the Rt. Rev. Robert E. Gribbin and the Rev. Boston M. Lackey from Western North Carolina; and the Rt. Rev. Edwin A. Penick and the Rev. John Long Jackson representing the Diocese of North Carolina.

In May, 1939 the committee recommended hiring "an expert" to make a survey of the institution and its operation. Mrs. Robert L. Duckworth, executive secretary of the Methodist Orphans' Home Association in St. Louis was hired through the Child Welfare League of America to conduct the survey between August and September of that year.

At the same May 18, 1939 Executive Committee meeting, superintendent William Wheeler offered his resignation, to make way for any administrative changes the Committee felt were necessary. His resignation was tabled, however, until completion of Mrs. Duckworth's survey.

Bishop Penick's special study committee reviewed an extensive list of recommendations submitted by Mrs. Duckworth on September 16, 1939, forming them into a proposal for the Board of Managers set to meet in January, 1940. Those recommendations included:

a. Hire a trained social service case worker.
b. Discontinue the office of business manager, effective May 1, 1940.
c. Formulate specific personnel policies relating to qualifications for employment, salary scale, vacations, sick leave, etc.
d. Study the cost of the farm and dairy operation.
e. Use married couples instead of matrons for cottages with older children in residence.
f. Add more bathing and toilet facilities to some cottages.
g. Provide individual towels, wash cloths and toilet articles with "definite training given in their daily use."
h. Establish a vacation fund so that every child may have an annual vacation.
i. Give each child a weekly allowance.
j. Broaden the recreational program.
k. Reorganize the training program so that "the educational values which exist in group life may be utilized for the benefit of the children."

l. Use the Mental Hygiene Clinic more frequently in meeting problems of unacceptable behavior.

m. Provide for semi-annual, rather than annual meetings, of the Board of Managers.

A final recommendation asked that William Wheeler be appointed the first orphanage chaplain and a new, trained superintendent be hired.

Two possible fields of specialized service were also suggested for the future development of the orphanage: a program of institutional and foster care; and vocational training and placement for dependent and neglected adolescents whose needs were not being met by other existing agencies.

All of the recommendations were adopted by the Board at their January 30, 1940 meeting. William Wheeler was appointed the first orphanage Chaplain, at a salary of $1,500 a year, and asked to serve as acting superintendent until the new superintendent arrived. By vote of the Board, Manly Dowell Whisnant, an Episcopal layman, was elected superintendent of the orphanage, and his wife, Pearl Berry Whisnant was elected supervising matron. They were to assume their new positions in July, 1940.

CLIMBING OUT OF DEPRESSION

M.D. Whisnant was the first layman elected to the post, and the first person to bring to the job a background in education. A native of Morganton, Whisnant attended Christ School in Arden and received his BA degree in education from the University of North Carolina in 1927. He had worked as athletic director for the Gastonia city schools and for the Hoosac School in New York, and as principal of Mt. Olive High School. When he was accepted for the position at Thompson Orphanage, he was principal of Belhaven (N.C.) High School.

Pearl Whisnant was a graduate of Brenau College in Gainesville, Georgia with a degree in physical education. She had also attended the University of North Carolina where she met her husband.

Both were tall, stately in carriage, athletic in build, and abounding in energy for the task ahead. Together, they painted a larger-than-life portrait for the children of Thompson Orphanage, a picture of what real parents could be.

The institution had climbed out of the Depression intact, though weary, and was eager to test its new resolve in the onrushing decade.

FOOTNOTES

1. Thomas C. Parramore and Douglas C. Wilms, *North Carolina: The History of an American State* (Englewood Cliffs, New Jersey: Prentice-Hall, Inc., 1983), p. 359.

2. Thomas C. Parramore, *Express Lanes and Country Roads: The Way We Lived In North Carolina, 1920-1970* (Chapel Hill: University of North Carolina Press, 1983), p. 20.

3. Tom E. Terrill and Jerrold Hirsch, eds., *Such as Us: Southern Voices of the Thirties* (Chapel Hill: University of North Carolina Press, 1978), p. 52.

4. "Minutes," Executive Committee September 16, 1930.

5. "Information for Four-Minute Speakers," 1934, Thompson Orphanage Historical Files, Charlotte, N.C.

6. Ibid.

7. "Minutes," Executive Committee, March 18, 1932.

8. "Minutes," Executive Committee, January 15, 1932.

9. John L. Bell, Jr., *Hard Times: Beginnings of the Great Depression in North Carolina, 1929-1933* (Raleigh: Division of Archives and History, North Carolina Department of Cultural Resources, 1982), p. 41.

10. "Minutes," Executive Committee, October 20, 1931.

11. "Minutes," Executive Committee, January 10, 1934.

12. "Bill Gordon Adds Appeal For Orphanage Offering," *The Carolina Churchman*, November 15, 1938, p. 2.

13. "Minutes," Executive Committee, September 18, 1934.

14. "Minutes," Executive Committee, June 21, 1938.

15. "Minutes," Executive Committee, April 18, 1933.

16. "Minutes," Executive Committee, November 19, 1935.

17. "Minutes," Executive Committee, March 15, 1938.

18. "Minutes," Executive Committee, April, 19, 1932.

19. Lillie Mae White, interview, March 9, 1985.

20. Ibid.

21. Ibid.

22. George Powell, interview, April 8, 1985.

23. Ibid.

24. Ibid.

25. Ibid.

26. Henry W. Crane, M.D. to William H. Wheeler, November 19, 1931, Thompson Orphanage Historical Files, Charlotte, N.C.

27. Claudia Hunter to Thompson Orphanage Executive Committee, November 19, 1931, Thompson Orphanage Historical Files, Charlotte, N.C.

28. Ibid.

29. Ibid.

30. "Minutes," Executive Committee, November 7, 1934.

31. George Powell, interview, April 8, 1985.

32. "Minutes," Executive Committee, October 26, 1937.

33. "Annual Report," January, 1937, p. 2.

34. Maude Waddell, "Thompson Orphanage Celebration To Be Glorious Spiritual Jubilee: 50 Years of Magnificent Christian Achievement," prepared for Thompson Orphanage Semi-Centennial Jubilee, May 7, 1937.

35. Ibid.

36. Milton A. Barber, "Great Trees from Little Acorns Grow," prepared for Thompson Orphanage Semi-Centennial Jubilee, May 7, 1937.

37. Ibid.

38. Ibid.

39. Francis O. Clarkson, "A Never Failing Succession of Benefactors," prepared for Thompson Orphanage Semi-Centennial Jubilee, May 7, 1937.

40. Ibid.

41. Edwin A. Penick, "Prayer For The Thompson Orphanage," Thompson Orphanage Historical Files, Charlotte, N.C.

42. "An Historical Pageant," Thompson Orphanage Semi-Centennial Jubilee, May 7, 1937.

43. "Celebration Is Held At Orphans' Home," *The Charlotte Observer,* May 8, 1937, p. 1.

44. "Our Song," Thompson Orphanage Semi-Centennial Jubilee, May 7, 1937.

45. "Minutes," Executive Committee, June 20, 1939.

46. "Minutes," Board of Managers, February 8, 1939.

47. Ibid.

Chapter 6

A Sense Of Family

1940 — 1955

When Manly Dowell Whisnant, nicknamed "Red" for his brilliant hair and gay profusion of freckles, took over supervision of the Thompson Orphanage in 1940, he inherited a bank balance of $143.23, debts of $4,685.42,[1] 63 acres of farmland left virtually abandoned, and a family of 87 children, each with different needs, goals and abilities. "The children themselves presented what appeared then to be a mountainous problem," said Whisnant looking back. "It wasn't a matter of just learning their names and ages. Children were all strangers — boys and girls of all ages and with personalities as different as heritage and early environment could make them."[2]

Red and Pearl Whisnant, who had no children of their own, made it clear from the first that the children living at the orphanage would be treated as their own; that with the presence of the superintendent's wife as supervising matron a new dimension would be added to the character and quality of the childrens' lives, a dimension which presented by example the role and function of parents. The Whisnants, who asked to be called simply "Pop" and "Mom"

quickly began shaping this collection of individuals they had inherited into a family.

And as the children discovered, there were both advantages and responsibilities involved in family living.

OUT IN THE FIELDS

When he wasn't at the bank borrowing money to help meet orphanage expenses, Pop was out in the fields with boys, joining them in the plowing, planting, and harvesting chores which were necessary to revitalize the farm. "I obtained a $35 mule and with the help of the boys we began to grow vegetables for table use,"[3] he explained. At first they concentrated on small vegetable gardens in back of the cottages. "Pretty soon, everybody was anxious to help," said Pop, mainly because of the improvements in the orphanage menu. "At this period we had meat once a week, we had eggs once a week," he said, "and we ate a lot of cereal and peanut butter."[4] By the Spring of 1941 the orphanage had an 8-acre garden producing green beans, corn, tomatoes, peas, onions, cabbage, okra, beets, carrots, cu-

cumbers, squash, peppers and assorted greens.

The dairy was also revitalized, providing more work for the boys, and milk and butter for the table. During the summer of 1942, several friends of the orphanage donated a tractor and plow to help bring the farm into full production, and another group of businessmen, headed by George M. Dowdy, raised funds to buy a herd of eight purebred Jersey cows from Charlotte's Morrocroft farm estate. Pop soon added to the herd until there was enough milk to supply the needs of the entire orphanage and a surplus to sell, which helped pay for the feed. A new barn for the dairy operation was constructed in 1943, replacing the one gutted by fire in 1939.

Early in 1942, the city had approached the orphanage with a proposal to purchase a six-acre tract of land bordering on Pearl Street to be used as a playground for Negro children. It wasn't until February, 1943, however, that the sale was approved, over the protests of some adjoining property owners. The $2,500 paid for the park land was placed in the permanent Endowment Fund. At the same time, the City also put a road through the orphanage property connecting Baxter and Stonewall streets. Neither of these changes, however, appeared to impede the progress of the farming and dairy activities on the campus.

CLEAN HAIR ON THURSDAY

Mrs. Whisnant quickly turned her attention toward instilling in the children a greater sense of responsibility using a system she and the cottage residents called the 'check and black mark chart.' Expectations, and duties, for each child were recorded on the chart posted in the cottage. Children, from the youngest to the oldest, were to dress themselves and make up their beds each morning, participate in the pre-breakfast prayer service in each cottage, then carry out certain assigned duties which could include sweeping, setting the table, cooking, or serving. They took baths every night and on Thursdays, everybody's hair was washed. Clothes were to be mended, with no rips or missing buttons, and lockers and drawers kept neat and tidy. The children watched the chart carefully to see if their duties were carried out satisfactorily, indicated by a check mark. Once or twice a week

they earned a special privilege if there were no black marks by their name. Privileges could be a movie, football or basketball game, a boxing match or a trip uptown.[5]

The children, beginning to settle into a new phase of orphanage life with Mom and Pop, expressed their feelings in a series of letters published by *The Charlotte News* in 1941:

> "We have about 75 children here and they take part in the different things that are done. The girls work in the laundry. The boys work in the field, cut wood and do odd jobs that come up. There are 41 girls here among which there are some very pretty ones." — Henry Swain, age 16.
>
> "We have a lovely big campus and lots and lots of trees. We also have a pony and cart. The pony's name is Peggy. We take turns riding her in the afternoon when we come home from school ... " — Betsy Boyd, age 11.
>
> "I am having a swell time. We have planted 11,000 collards and 3,500 cabbages. We have a pony, three mules, five heifers and five bulls.
>
> "We are cutting wood and putting it in the two kindling houses. My house mother's name is Mrs. Leech. When I do what I am told not to do I get a spanking. I have lived out here a long time and I think it is a swell place. I want to live out here until I finish school." — George Williams, age 11.

A SWELL PLACE

The new superintendent, the Board and Executive Committee performed considerable financial balancing acts behind the scenes in order to provide such "a swell place" for the children. Facing the all-too-familiar prospect of insufficient income to meet mounting expenses, Red Whisnant became a familiar figure at the local bank's loan department during the early 1940's. One of his first official acts as superintendent of the orphanage was to borrow $7,000 to keep it in business. He also closed two of the cottages to help lower expenses.[6]

In January, 1941 Lawrence E. Watt, finance chairman, presented a comprehensive study of orphanage finances, showing that income had at one time been around $30,000 annually, that it had declined considerably during the Depression and while it had risen some, it was still not

A familiar sight: "Mom" Whisnant surrounded by children.

sufficient for the needs. Regular income received during 1940 was $24,301.93; the amount spent, $28,658.20.[7]

In his report to the Board in June, 1941, Whisnant discussed the current operating budget of $32,025 which was "somewhat higher than for the last few years, though not as large as the time before the Depression."[8] Much of the increase came from salaries paid to new orphanage personnel including a general handyman, the chaplain William H. Wheeler, and a full-time caseworker, Miss D'Anna. To meet these and other expenses, the orphanage counted on several sources of income: slightly less than $2,000 a year from The Duke Endowment; about $1,000 annually from the orphanage Endowment Fund; $1,000 a year from county support or from parents; and about $20,000 from the churches, either from the Thanksgiving offering, the diocesan budget, or from individual or church contributions throughout the year. By year's end, Whisnant reported more cheerfully, "We only borrowed $6,000."[9]

Red Whisnant became less of a 'familiar figure' at the bank loan desk after 1942 when the Executive Committee established a sustaining fund designed to help the institution run on "a more substantial as well as a more economical basis without damaging the health and wholesome life of the children and those employed by the institution."[10] The sustaining fund was divided in 1944 into a revolving fund which was held in reserve until needed, and a building and improvement fund for permanent improvements. The money received, borrowed, and repaid into these accounts added greater efficiency in financial planning and management.

There was greater efficiency, too, in the area of social service planning with the hiring of a full-time social worker "whose services assure us through careful investigation," explained Whisnant, "that the children whom we do admit are in real need of our care; and that those whom we do not take can find that care with the family or some other type of assistance."[11] There was an evident increase in the number of applications for admission by 1943, attributed in part to the separation of families caused by the nation's entry into World War II. Enough children were admitted to allow the cottages closed in 1940 to reopen, greatly relieving overcrowding in Baker Cottage. Miss Grace Woodruff, who took over the social work position in 1942, served only a short time, following which Pearl Whisnant assumed the additional responsibilities of case work.

During all discussions of economy and budget, Red Whisnant stressed the importance of the orphanage farm.

> I believe that our real salvation lies in operating our farm . . . The sixty-three acres of land that we have will almost take care of our food bill, if it is operated as it should be. Too, we need it as a training program. Children must have something to keep them busy. This program should be a balanced one. Some work and some play, not all of either. That is the kind of program that I am carrying forward.[12]

ALUMNI ASSOCIATION FORMED

The idea of 'family' which the Whisnants worked so hard to achieve was given a boost in 1943 with the formal organization of the Thompson Orphanage Alumni Association. The result of an informal group of graduates living in Charlotte, the Alumni Association was designed to keep old family ties strong while giving the present orphanage residents a unique type of heritage. Thomas J. Myers, an orphanage graduate who left his study of medicine at the University of North Carolina to enlist in the Marine Corps at the start of WWII, was instrumental in the association's founding, but he never got to attend a reunion. He was killed in Okinawa on May 15, 1945, one of three orphanage graduates who lost their lives during that war.

Others were Herbert Hobbs and Harold Cook. Baker Cottage cook Lillie Mae White remembered the day Harold Cook left "to go off to the war. He came in and gave me a five-dollar bill and kind'a choked and asked me to pray for him. He didn't come back."[13]

Fellow orphanage graduate Bill Gatlin, a student at North Carolina State University, described the alumni's feeling of loss:

> The boys who played ball so spiritedly and classically on this campus, griped about working, studying, and restrictions, never considered themselves as warriors for Uncle Sam or especially honored heroes. Lean, healthy adolescents, self-consciously perched on top of a returning hay wagon with their sun-tanned backs bared to the Fourth Street traffic, knew themselves to be just plain ordinary kids enjoying a wholesome living.[14]

And despite the war, the Thompson Orphanage family of children continued to be "just plain, ordinary kids." They had chores and responsibilities like most other children, for which they received an allowance, they played hard, participated in all kinds of sports and social activities, established strong friendships, and, for the most part, took pride in the Thompson Orphanage as their home.

FEW WAR RIPPLES

Compared to the Depression of the prior decade, World War II went virtually unnoticed on the Thompson Orphanage campus. While families throughout the city counted their ration stamps and gave up all thoughts of eating meat, except maybe on Sunday, the children at the institution enjoyed a bountiful harvest of their own farm produce, including eggs, milk, chicken, beef, and pork. The orphanage also received a supplementary sugar ration. Gas rationing

had little effect either; nearly everything the family needed was either on the property or within walking distance. A certain "unrest" was detected among the older children which Whisnant attributed to the war and an increasing national tendency toward "juvenile delinquency."[15]

About the only real evidence of war's inconvenience came during construction of a new central dining room and kitchen. This new addition to the administration building, begun in the summer of 1944, was expected to take only six months to finish. But war restrictions and shortages of material delayed completion until June 4, 1945 when the first meal was served in the new facility. The dining room was actually the remodeled kindergarten room, but the adjoining kitchen was an entirely new structure built just in back of the dining room and along the side of the gym. It had a large butler's pantry, the main kitchen, a quick freeze room, two refrigeration rooms and a large storage area. In the kitchen were three sinks, a large gas stove, an electric potato peeler and, most treasured of all, a huge dishwasher.

Beginning his report to the Board in February, 1946, Red Whisnant praised the support of orphanage benefactors which "has resulted in a program of achievement and advancement, placing our institution in a position to give our children a well-balanced life now and prepare them to meet the daily tasks of life."[16] It appeared that as the nation emerged victorious from World War II, the institution had shaken itself free of cyclical borrowing and was operating from a much firmer financial base. During 1947 contributions to the Endowment Fund topped $100,000 and the operating budget exceeded $53,000. At year's end there was still money in the bank.

FAMILY TRADITIONS

The institution's central dining hall, more than a physical improvement, was a demonstration of the Whisnant's belief in the importance of bringing the children together as a family unit. Mom and Pop ate there too, switching tables to share each meal with a different group of children. The dining room soon became the center for celebrations and a place where memories were made, and shared.

Birthdays were particularly joyous times. During boisterous renditions of "Happy Birthday to You", a cake would be presented to the birthday child, to be shared with fellow cottage residents. And everyone got ice cream. "We also got to give a piece of cake to anyone else we wanted,"[17] recalled Stella Henson, who came to the orphanage in 1945. On her sixteenth birthday, Henson walked across the room to give her boyfriend a special piece of birthday cake, growing redder and redder in the face as the other children chanted, "Sweet sixteen and never been kissed — or has she?!"

Bishop Edwin Penick received similar treatment in 1953 when he happened to share a meal, on his birthday, with the orphanage youngsters. He was surprised with the cake, but perhaps even more so with the song, to which he gaily replied, "I haven't been kissed half enough and that's for sure!"[18]

There were other important rituals, too. Each school morning Pop Whisnant walked with a gaggle of children to the corner of Fourth Street and Kings Drive, where he kissed each goodbye

and watched them safely across the street. There the children headed off in various directions to Central High, Piedmont or Elizabeth schools and later to Garinger High. Clutched tightly in each child's hand was a paper sack lunch, prepared, often before daylight, in the central kitchen. Mary Froebe, who also came to the orphanage in 1945 remembered, "When I was on duty in the dining hall, we made about 500 sandwiches a day."[19]

As concerned parents of Charlotte's largest family of school-aged children, Pop and Mom attended all Parent-Teacher Association meetings, and signed each child's report card. "They treated us as individuals," said Mary Froebe. "They knew what each of us was capable of doing and always offered encouragement."[20]

Encouragement came, too, from the alumni association which began a program of scholastic achievement and citizenship awards in 1945. All children who maintained an 'A', 'B', or 'C' average in school received a cash award, supplied by donations from association members. Presentation of the awards soon became an eagerly anticipated high point of the annual reunions.

Older girls helped serve meals in the central dining hall.

"Pop" Whisnant sees the kids off to school.

"Some years it nearly broke us," declared Ben Nash, alumni association treasurer since the group's inception. "But, the more the merrier."[21]

As in years past, the Christmas holiday held a particular significance for the children at Thompson Orphanage. Their wish lists of three to five gifts each were almost always met, to the letter. Contributions of toys, food, clothing and money from Episcopal churches, auxiliaries and other friends of the orphanage helped make the holiday a joyous celebration.

"Mom and her secretary would wrap all the gifts that hadn't already come wrapped," explained Stella Henson. "Then on Christmas Eve the big boys and girls put them under the tree in each cottage." In some cottages, depending on the routine of the matron, children could rush downstairs on Christmas morning and immediately open their gifts. Others had to wait anxiously through breakfast.

There was always a service in the Chapel, followed by a big Christmas dinner, but the high point of the day was going to Mom's and Pop's home and crowding around the enormous tree in their living room. Lillie Mae White vividly remembered this Christmas tradition, because she and Pop had to move a heavy sofa upstairs every year to make room for 'Mom's tree'. "Every year it was the same thing," she chuckled. "I could hear him mumbling and complaining about having to move it, but I didn't dare say anything."[22]

Around the tree were all the dolls in Mom's collection, and Pop's electric trains. And underneath, a present from the Whisnants for every child, very often a book of theater tickets which were put into use that afternoon. "Christmas Day afternoons were the loneliest days of the year," admitted Stella Henson.[23] They were times when even the Whisnant's best efforts at creating family ties couldn't substitute for the real thing.

"THEY LOOK LIKE THEIR FATHER"

One of Pearl Whisnant's innovations as supervising matron was an individualized plan for buying clothes, as they were needed rather than all at one time. Auxiliaries in all three dioceses 'adopted' specific children at the orphanage with a pledge to supply their necessary clothing. In return, auxiliary members received a snapshot of the child, and plenty of grateful smiles.

The youngsters were also treated to two major clothes shopping trips each year: in the Spring, for Easter outfits, and in the Fall for school clothes. The girls, especially, seemed to enjoy the group trips to downtown Charlotte's Belk department store, where, with Mom's assistance, they could buy a Palm Sunday dress and an Easter dress, hat, shoes, and even gloves. "We always had nice clothes," declared Stella Henson.

"The only thing I never did like was going in groups," she said. "I never kept a secret of my living at the orphanage, but when we were all in a group I felt like people would be saying, 'Well, here come the orphans, poor little things.' "[24]

What most people said to Pearl Whisnant, when she was out shopping with a group of eight or ten youngsters, was an inevitable, "Are all these children yours? They don't look like you," to which she would reply, "They look like their father!"[25] She obviously enjoyed the shopping trips, and tried to stay up with current styles. "You know pink and black are such stylish colors for boys this year," she once commented. "I almost got run down trying to get pink ties and socks."[26]

A NEW FARM

Red Whisnant had revived the orphanage farm to such an extent that by 1945 the Executive Committee began considering the possible purchase of "a farm in the country." At the March 20, 1945 meeting, a committee was appointed to study potential development of the institution and the need for such a farm. By July, the Executive Committee unanimously agreed to recommend to the Board of Managers the purchase from the Soules family of Cedarbrook Farm, consisting of 169.61 acres in Morningstar Township, about 8 miles from the campus.

The orphanage paid $75 an acre for the property, or a total of $12,720.75. The purchase was made possible by consent of the Diocese of East Carolina to use money left in its building fund, plus the proceeds from the sale of the property for the Pearl Street Park, and the donation of $1,000 by "a friend." Horace Davis, who acted as real estate agent for the orphanage, also donated his commission toward the purchase.

In a report to the Executive Committee on September 17, 1945, Whisnant appealed for funds to "buy hogs, hens, some beef cattle, a ton and a half truck, and to make some repairs." He was allowed to borrow $1,000 from the revolving fund to stock the new farm with hogs and chickens. And friends of the orphanage again came with gifts: a herd of beef cattle, four cows and a bull, from George Poston of Gastonia, and ten hogs from Dr. and Mrs. E.R. Hipp of Charlotte. A new farm was in business.

The 1945 Thanksgiving Offering appeal gave a kids'-eye-view of the Cedarbrook purchase:

> You would probably like to see what we are doing with our new farm, Cedarbrook, which you bought this past year. When the Board said to go ahead and get it, they were thinking of what a good investment it would be — a place to raise chickens and eggs, big pastures for our own beef cattle, an orchard al-

A traditional Christmas.

ready planted with a variety of fruit, and even a pond to stock with fish. But we girls and boys had some different ideas — weekends in the country, picnics in the woods, even our own swimming hole.

The farm was both a resource for food supplies and a special haven for recreation, hunting, and fishing. Summer Sunday afternoons were always reserved for swimming, usually followed by a picnic supper or a fish fry down by the lake. The boys stayed busy planting and harvesting, both at the in-town farm and at Cedarbrook, and the girls spent many a summer day helping to can, freeze and preserve the produce. Of course, the girls could help with the farm work too. "Picking strawberries was always fun," remembered Mary Froebe, "because if you found a double berry you got to kiss Pop!"[27]

GIFTS FROM HOLLYWOOD

A large boat used on one of the new farm's lakes was donated by Hollywood movie star Rod Cameron, who took a special interest in the Thompson Orphanage children after his first visit during a Charlotte rodeo in 1948.[28] He tried

A pair of contented 4-H Award winners.

to visit the orphanage at least once a year, and remembered each child with gifts at Christmas and on their birthdays. "One of my most pleasant memories," said Mary Froebe, "is of cornhusking in the Fall, and I can remember I wore a flannel shirt from Rod Cameron."[29] He also interested other personalities from the motion picture industry in sending gifts to the children. " . . . I have visited hundreds of orphanages all over the country and have never been in one that was as well run or where the kids were as nice and well mannered as they are at Thompson, so I feel that they are deserving of all the help they get from myself and others," Cameron explained in a handwritten note to Bishop Edwin Penick.[30]

In August, 1952, Rod Cameron presented the Whisnants with a $1,000 check to set up an educational fund for orphanage boys and girls who wanted to attend college, and he pledged to add a similar sum each year. Known as the Rod Cameron Educational Fund, it helped fulfill a long-standing need for additional funds to aid orphanage students in continuing their education in vocational, business or college courses and came just a few weeks after a similar gift made by Anthony J. Gocking of Charlotte establishing the Minnie L. Gocking Memorial College Educational Fund.

CONTENTED COWS, FRANTIC TRAFFIC

After the purchase of Cedarbrook Farm, the Board of Managers laid the groundwork in January, 1949 for future real estate holdings, agreeing to amend the charter and increase the amount of real and personal property the institution could hold from "an amount not to exceed one million dollars," to "unlimited amount and value."[31]

The value of the orphanage land, within a few blocks of Charlotte's City Hall, became an increasingly potent factor in determining the future direction of the institution. Everyone, it seemed, wanted a slice of the corn fields and pastures, but not for corn or milk.

On January 21, 1948, the Board of Managers granted the State Highway and Public Works Commission a right-of-way of 120 feet for State Highway Project 6556, and received $7,500 as compensation. Completed between 1950-1951, the six-lane Independence Boulevard came in at the back end of Cecil Street, crossed Sugar Creek and split in half what the children used to call the "glass field" because of all the broken glass continually churned up in this corn field. Kenilworth Avenue also came up Sugar Creek from Morehead to meet Independence Boulevard, crowding in on the orphanage property. The children used a culvert to reach the fields on the far side of Independence, and the cows grazed unconcerned just a few yards from the passing traffic.

Faced with steady encroachment on all sides, the orphanage again set its sights on country property, authorizing in January, 1951 the purchase of the James Farm, also in Morningstar Township and across from the Cedarbrook property. The 130-acre plot cost a total of $23,750. Combined with Cedarbrook, the James Farm purchase brought the institution's holdings in the country to 300 acres. "This investment is not only good from a money viewpoint," explained Executive Committee chairman R. H. Bouligny, "but it is a good insurance against future complications."[32]

Thompson Orphanage had earlier turned down an offer of 200 acres of land in Monroe, proposed as a gift by Vernon Lockhart on the stipulation that the institution operate at least one cottage or building on the property. The distance between the Charlotte campus and Monroe was considered too great to make the offer feasible.

Rod Cameron

Movie Star Rod Cameron visits with the orphanage children.

A UNIQUE LANDMARK

"The prize-winning herd of Jersey cows grazing at the city's geographic heart within five blocks of City Hall may be Charlotte's most unique landmark . . . "[33] claimed *The Charlotte Observer* in 1952. Motorists at the traffic light at Independence Boulevard and Baldwin Circle were invited to "gaze and wonder and admire" the view of orphanage pasture land which had suddenly become a sought-after commercial property, estimated in worth between $500,000 and one million dollars exclusive of buildings, livestock or equipment.[34]

Thompson Orphanage received numerous offers from city government, industry and business, to purchase portions of its urban farm. The City of Charlotte proposed such an offer in 1950, seeking ten acres as a site for an auditorium-coliseum. While remaining open to the possibility of selling its property, R. H. Bouligny pointed out that the orphanage was in many ways "ideally situated" close to urban schools, churches, cultural and entertainment facilities yet providing "the wholesome advantages of farm living."[35]

Should the institution look toward developing at another site, possibly using the newly-acquired farms in the country? Should the city property be sold or leased? Could Thompson Orphanage continue to provide its services to needy children at its present urban location? To help answer some of these questions, Bishop Edwin Penick appointed two committees in 1953: one to study the best use of the property located within the city; the other to consider removal of the orphanage to another site.

The committee examining uses for the city property proposed developing approximately seven acres as a retail shopping complex, to be managed by the orphanage. Details of the plan were revealed in the September 3, 1953 edition of *The Charlotte Observer:*

> The layout planned by the committee calls for buildings facing Independence Blvd. and Baldwin Cir. with large parking areas in front of each structure. The buildings planned are a service station at Independence Blvd. and Baldwin Cir., a supermarket with big parking areas on both of these streets, a drugstore, a hardware store, a variety store, a beauty parlor, a barber shop, a shoe repair shop, a doctor's office and a branch bank building.[36]

There were those who had serious reservations about the project, including M. George Henry, Bishop of the Diocese of Western North Carolina. " . . . Is it quite right for the Church to be so far involved in the real estate business?" he asked.[37] "Are we, in the next ten years, involving ourselves in a program ten or twenty times as large as this first step?"[38] After more intense study of the high cost of financing and managing the project, the Board of Managers abandoned the plan.

But the idea of a shopping center did not die. One of the many offers brought before the Board came from Thomas Alexander of Younts Realty Company who represented two interested syndicates who wanted to either buy or lease for a long term the land on the south side of the orphanage property for a shopping center. Negotiations continued from the initial contact in January, 1951 through 1954, culminating in November, 1954 with the announcement in *The Charlotte Observer,* "Orphanage Tract Is Leased For Huge Shopping Center." James W. Rouse and Company of Baltimore leased a 50-acre tract of land stretching from East Fourth Street across Independence Boulevard, and running on either side at Baldwin Circle to a point almost halfway between Independence and East Morehead Street for development of Charlotte's first enclosed shopping center, to be called Charlottetown Mall. The lease, as negotiated with the Rouse Company, was to run for 99 years, with a minimum rental of $50,000 a year beginning after the third year. Total cost of the shopping center was estimated at $5,000,000.

R. H. Bouligny, chairman of the special committee which conducted the lease negotiations for the orphanage, explained, "Thompson Orphanage and Training Institution will continue to occupy the approximately 10 acres on which the orphanage buildings are now located. This will be for an indefinite length of time until plans can be developed at some future time for possible removal of the Orphanage to a new site."[39] Rental money was allocated to the building fund for a new orphanage and would not affect current operating expenses.

FALSE PROSPERITY

No sooner had the lease agreement been signed than the orphanage began to feel the sting of 'false prosperity.' Just three weeks following the announcement, Red Whisnant said, "We have already noticed less interest in contributing."[40] He was quick to point out that the institution was not "rolling in money. We still need a great deal of help."[41]

Generous donors, interested citizens, casual passersby point to the 4th St. location and smile. These boys, they say, are doing all

right. It just isn't so. The plight of the institution is not much better now than it ever has been. If anything, the situation there has been complicated ... Next year's budget is $85,000 and the prospect of meeting it is slim.[42]

Other factors, too, influenced the level of giving in November, 1954, such as 'Hurricane Hazel' which ripped across the eastern part of the state and diverted some charitable contributions in that diocese. But none were so devastating, or tricky to deal with, than the notion that Thompson Orphanage was suddenly rich.

An aerial photo of Charlotte taken in 1956 outlines Thompson's property before construction of the Charlottetown Mall.

COMING HOME

When over 70 alumni came "home" for their reunion in 1955, the edge of expectancy was sharp. They knew this time might be their last to see the orphanage as they'd always known it. Independence Boulevard already looked like a smooth scar scoring the once rural pasture which held so many memories, "of crop planting and harvesting, grazing and milking cows, trapping rabbits and muskrats, swimming in Sugar Creek, and other childhood pranks."[43] Soon it would all be gone, replaced with a multi-million dollar shopping complex.

The year 1955 was unsettling in many ways. It was the year teenage boys in dungarees hid copies of 'Lolita' under their school notebooks while girls, puffed up by layers of crinolines, cried over James Dean in 'Rebel Without A Cause.' On the other side of the globe, civil war churned in an obscure country called Vietnam. And in the United States, IBM Corporation shipped out its first business computer.

Charles Kuralt, a young reporter for *The Charlotte News* who had not yet been called 'on the road,' was sent to cover the annual reunion of Thompson Orphanage alumni on June 12, 1955 and filed this report for the next day's edition:

> They came back to Thompson Orphanage yesterday.
> From New York and Memphis and Charlotte they came — the orphanage kids, now grown up — back to the 'old home-place.'

They brought their families with them. They played ball and milked the cows and spread a picnic supper, just as many of them did years ago. They shook each other's hands and walked the sprawling green grounds that once had been the center of their lives . . .

One of the returnees, J.H. 'Cy' Dillon of Charlotte sat on the steps of the old chapel talking to Diane Devier, a new girl at the orphanage.

'There used to be a pot-bellied stove in this chapel,' Mr. Dillion remembered. 'We used to fire it up every Sunday morning before church.' . . .

The returning alumni noted many changes at the orphanage. Mrs. Era Mae Walick of Burlington was surprised to see bustling Independence Boulevard cutting through the old pasture.

'But the biggest difference,' said John L. Fort, now head of his own Charlotte advertising company, 'is in the psychology. We were in an institution back in the 20's. And most of us were ashamed of it. It's not an institution any more. It's a home; the kids know it better than anybody.' . . .

James Bond of Memphis, Tenn., was making his first reunion since he left the orphanage in 1934. His wife was seeing for the first time the place he spent his childhood.

'I see there's a big rose bush gone from the front yard,' Mr. Bond said. 'But things haven't really changed so much.'

He pointed to some boys playing ball on the lawn.

'We could knock a softball from here down to the church. And you know, I saw a boy do it just a minute ago.'[44]

FOOTNOTES

1. "Annual Report," January 23, 1953.

2. Ibid.

3. "Semi-Annual Report," June 27, 1957.

4. Ibid.

5. Annie Mae Brown, "A Day At The Orphanage: Boys & Girls At Thompson Are Taught To Think For Themselves," *The Charlotte News,* circa 1941, clipping from Thompson Orphanage Historical Files, Charlotte, N.C.

6. M.D. Whisnant to Edwin A. Penick, July 16, 1942, Edwin A. Penick Papers, Thompson Orphanage, 1920-1949, Diocesan House, Raleigh, N.C.

7. "Minutes," Board of Managers, January 30, 1941.

8. "Semi-Annual Report," June 18, 1941, p. 1.

9. M.D. Whisnant to Edwin A. Penick, July 16, 1942.

10. "Minutes," Executive Committee, January 12, 1942.

11. "Semi-Annual Report," June 18, 1941, p. 1.

12. M.D. Whisnant to Edwin A. Penick, July 16, 1942.

13. Kays Gary, "Her 'Children' Never Forget Lillie Mae," *The Charlotte Observer,* October 10, 1976, p. 1B.

14. *Thompson Orphanage Alumni Association Newsletter,* July 4, 1945, p. 2.

15. "Minutes," Executive Committee, April 13, 1943.

16. "Minutes," Board of Managers, February 6, 1946.

17. Stella Henson, interview, April 27, 1985.

18. "Pop and Mom's Column", *Alumni Association Newsletter,* Summer, 1954, p. 3.

19. Mary Froebe, interview, March 16, 1985.

20. Ibid.

21. Ben Nash, interview, April 10, 1985.

22. Lillie Mae White, interview, March 9, 1985.

23. Stella Henson, interview, March 27, 1985.

24. Ibid.

25. Hannah Miller, "Thompson Orphanage Heart Pounds With Love And Pride As Another Birthday Arrives," *The Charlotte Observer,* March 4, 1962, p. 1D.

26. "Pop and Mom's Column," *Alumni Association Newsletter,* Summer, 1955, p. 4.

27. Mary Froebe, interview, March 16, 1985.

28. "Thompson Orphanage: 'Built Through Love'," *The Charlotte News,* February 24, 1962, p. 6B.

29. Mary Froebe, interview, March 16, 1985.

30. Rod Cameron to Bishop Edwin A. Penick, undated, Edwin A. Penick Papers, Thompson Orphanage, 1950-1959, Diocesan House, Raleigh, N.C.

31. "Certificate Of Amendment To The Charter Of The Thompson Orphanage And Training Institution," January 26, 1949, Edwin A. Penick Papers, Thompson Orphanage, 1920-1949, Diocesan House, Raleigh, N.C.

32. R.H. Bouligny to Edwin A. Penick, March 18, 1950, Edwin A. Penick Papers, Thompson Orphanage, 1950-1959, Diocesan House, Raleigh, N.C.

33. Randolph Norton, "Farm In Heart Of Charlotte Is Heart Of Good Citizenship," *The Charlotte Observer,* circa 1952, clipping in Thompson Orphanage Historical Files, Charlotte, N.C.

34. Ibid.

35. Ibid.

36. Hazel M. Trotter, "Thompson Orphanage Plans Extensive Business Section," *The Charlotte Observer,* September 3, 1953, p. 1B.

37. M. George Henry to Edwin A. Penick, July 2, 1953, Edwin A. Penick Papers, Thompson Orphanage, 1950-1959, Diocesan House, Raleigh, N.C.

38. Ibid.

39. Roy Covington, "Orphanage Tract Is Leased For Huge Shopping Center," *The Charlotte Observer,* November 23, 1954, p. 1B.

40. Julian Scheer, "Orphanage Not Cash-Heavy," *The Charlotte News,* December 10, 1954, sec. 2, p.1.

41. Ibid.

42. Ibid.

43. "Thompson Alumni to review year of transition," *Alumni Association Newsletter,* May, 1959, p. 1.

44. Charles Kuralt, "Thompson Alumni Return," *The Charlotte News,* June 13, 1955, pp. 1B, 16B.

Chapter 7

In Search Of Direction

1955 — 1965

Sara Holshouser knew all along she would win the Merchant's Association contest, not because her letter was so well-written, but because it was about her 'Pop.' As soon as she had heard about the Father's Day contest she knew this was her opportunity to express that very special relationship she, and 84 other children at Thompson Orphanage, shared with Pop Whisnant. The rules specified a short letter on the topic, "I Like My Dad Because . . . " Sara's only problem was keeping the many 'becauses' down to a manageable length of 50 words.

Sara fussed more over the scarf tied neatly at her neck for today's ceremony than she did in composing the award-winning letter. The words had come straight from the heart, and flowed easily through the pen.

Sara Holshouser and her Pop made a splendid pair as they appeared for the presentation of their prizes. Pop's thinning red hair, usually smothered beneath a battered straw hat, fell into its combed rows as neatly as a well-planted corn field and his cheery eyes, magnified behind rimless glasses, winked in approval as Sara accepted the $30 check, her first prize award, from J. Craig

Shelton of the Merchants' Association. Pop's sunburned face turned slightly more scarlet as Shelton then presented him with a $125 gift certificate for a new summer wardrobe. Glancing down at his worn lapels and frayed cuffs, Whisnant chuckled, wondering if it was his prize which had prompted Sara to enter him in the contest in the first place. Sara returned her 'father's' grin amid a flurry of popping flashbulbs. The local newspapers were making quite a stir over the story: a man with no children nominated Charlotte's Ideal Father for 1955 by a 16-year old orphan.

Sara sucked in her breath, her shoulders rising slightly as she prepared to read her letter aloud. With one hand resting in the firm, reassuring grip of her Pop, Sara read: "I like my dad because DAD, 'Pop' Whisnant, takes so much reponsibility caring for us and loves every minute of it. He is the most wonderful dad of 85 children in the world, with God's help. He works so hard, but is never too busy to advise and help us. That's my Dad."

The ancient Greeks believed that we do not face the future, rather we face the past while the future comes rushing on us from behind.[1] In a sense, that is how things happened for M.D. and Pearl Whisnant, and the Thompson Orphanage, during the decade 1955-1965. These were years in which the orphanage, while appearing to bow to the pressures of a more modern age, still functioned as a carefree anachronism.

WHERE DO WE GO FROM HERE?

There was a time of intense waiting between the first announcement in November, 1954 of the Rouse Company's intended development of a shopping mall on orphanage property, and the final exercise of the company's option on the land in August, 1956. But far from bringing clarity to the institution's plans, the lease arrangement with the Rouse Company created myriad questions to be studied, and a tremendous load of responsibility for the special planning committee appointed in 1952 by Bishop Edwin A. Penick to study relocation of the orphanage to another site.

Among the questions raised were: Is the country property the best location for the institution? Should the farming operation, especially the dairy, be continued or abandoned? Will there continue to be a need for institutional child care? What changes should be made in the institution's management, administration, and approach to child welfare to ensure its continued effectiveness? An equally knotty problem was presented by the orphanage's appearance of wealth juxtaposed with its very real need to increase charitable giving to support operating expenses.

"Everywhere I go," remarked Red Whisnant in his 1956 annual report, "people start telling me about how rich we are and that because of this fabulous wealth, we should not need any help."[2] It became imperative for the orphanage to emphasize that all money from the property rental was to be held in trust by the Trustees of the Diocese of North Carolina, and to accumulate for capital improvements anticipated in rebuilding the facility on the farm property. "If we don't get this idea to the public, the Thompson Orphanage will be regarded as a wealthy institution that no longer has a claim upon the interest and generosity of the public," said Board chairman, Bishop Edwin A. Penick.[3] The superinten-

dent used every opportunity to stress to contributors the necessity of continued support:

> Having always been a poor boy financially and having worked most of my life with destitute children I have just recently learned how detrimental wealth can be to the poor. . . . This money is being held in a Building Fund. We know that it will cost more than a million dollars to rebuild the orphanage on a new site. We intend to borrow the money using this lease as security. You do not have to be much of a mathematician to know that the interest rate of such a loan will just about use the $50,000 each year. Therefore, for current expenses we get no help from the lease and your responsibility as a contributor to the support of the Thompson Orphanage will continue as is as the years go by.[4]

The Thanksgiving Offering collected in 1956 was $32,960.62; the following year it dipped only slightly, to $32,469.55. However, said Whisnant in his report on the year 1957, "We have not recovered from the misunderstanding in the minds of many of our supporters that we are rich."[5]

R. H. Bouligny, chairman of the special planning committee, reiterated the problem in his report to the Diocesan Convention in Salisbury during May, 1957:

> A new home may have to be built — and at current costs! It is hoped that the Tenant's development will be successful and will provide sufficient money for those purposes. But there is one thing of which we may be assured — and that is — that it will be many, many years before any rental can be used in the actual operation of the Orphanage. During those years Red and Pearl and the Orphanage children must continue to look to the generosity of the Episcopalians in North Carolina for their support and maintenance.[6]

With the Rouse Company's promise that it would not take immediate possession of the land, but would give the superintendent four weeks notice before grading began, the special planning committee resumed with greater intensity its study of removing the orphanage to another site. The farm property at Cedarbrook, still considered the most logical site for relocation, was surveyed and contour maps made. Committee members then joined the superintendent in visiting other institutions including Oxford and Barium Springs orphanages in

North Carolina, and Spring Meadow Orphanage in Middletown, Kentucky, where they collected new ideas and concepts "on modern day methods of building institutions."[7]

At Bishop Edwin Penick's request, the committee secured professional advice from the Group Child Care Project of the Southeastern Conference of Workers in Children's Homes and the School of Social Work at the University of North Carolina. Dr. Alan Keith-Lucas and Alton M. Broten, representing the Group Child Care Project, conducted an on-site study January 28-30, and February 20-22, 1957, examining the current programs of Thompson Orphanage and assessing future options in terms of recognized trends within the field of child welfare, namely: a marked decrease in the number of orphans and half-orphans in the child population; increases in the total child population; the numbers of children involved in broken homes, those in trouble in juvenile courts, and orphaned and unwanted children placed for adoption; greater use of foster family homes; and a gradual decrease in the number of children cared for in childrens' institutions.

A FAMILY PORTRAIT

During the survey, consultants interviewed staff members and children at the orphanage, and observed daily routines. Through their findings emerged a revealing portrait of life at Thompson Orphanage:

"Thompson Orphanage has directed its service toward the care of children who must live away from home because of the death of one or both parents. It has not been set up to work much with parents ... "[8]

"The primary focus throughout ... has been upon the child."[9]

"Very few children within the institution were affiliated with the Episcopal Church before they were admitted."[10]

"Administrative staff has been kept at a minimum, with the superintendent and his wife sharing the responsibility."[11]

"The superintendent ... has an affection and interest in children and shows a particular knack in understanding them and in working directly with them in their daily lives."[12]

"Heat for the buildings is from the central plant, although a wood burning stove in each cottage is used for heating water ... Considerable emphasis is placed upon order and cleanliness in the cottages."[13]

"Most of the children, except the older high school boys, have their noon lunch at school and take bag lunches from the home. The older boys come to the institution to eat and then assist with washing dishes."[14]

"The Orphanage maintains an infirmary on the campus. It ... is under the supervision of a licensed practical nurse. She coordinates the medical and dental work that is done and gives most of the first aid ... For hospital care, Memorial Hospital is used and provides care at a cost discount of 20 percent. St. Peter's Foundation of a local Episcopal Church helps also with the cost of hospital care for the children."[15]

"Junior and senior boys help with the care and milking of 26 Jersey cows. This takes about 45 minutes in the morning and the same length of time in the afternoon each day of the week. Milking is done by hand ... Occasionally, a girl desires the opportunity to learn to milk and this has been arranged ... The Orphanage pasteurizes its own milk. The superintendent's goal has been to have one cow for each boy, ten years and older."[16]

"One of the main responsibilities of the girls on the campus is to assist with the laundry ... Most of the institution work is done on Monday. The girls do their own laundry on Tuesday. This work is done in the afternoons after school."[17]

"The Orphanage conducts no organized recreation program ... The ball field has deteriorated and has fallen into disuse. Sidewalks offer a limited opportunity for roller skating. The gym, which is small, is not used except for storage. Opportunities for recreation have been developed more on the farm, with the construction of the lodge, lakes for swimming, and the overnight house."[18]

"Considerable pride is taken in the appearance of the children ... Each child is sponsored by a church auxiliary which is asked to contribute $70.80 per year in cash. The Orphanage prefers to purchase the clothing ... These groups also help in remembering birthdays, Christmas, graduation, and vacations."[19]

"Each Friday, each child receives an

allowance, from 10 cents to 25 cents, depending upon his age. Special money is given for church or school projects."[20]

"Each houseparent receives one day off per week, from 10 a.m. to 10 p.m. . . . Salary scale for houseparents is from $100 to $125."[21]

THE BROTEN REPORT

The study, referred to as 'The Broten Report' predicted "institutions providing services which are geared to areas of great need will continue to be in high demand." Those needs identified in the report included care for children from broken homes, those emotionally disturbed or mentally and/or physically handicapped, those in need of shelter or emergency care, special minority or racial groups, and delinquent children. Specifically, the report suggested three possible alternatives for Thompson Orphanage: 1. to relocate its present program to a new facility, continuing to offer its services primarily to orphans and half-orphans in need of long term residential care, realizing that the numbers of true orphans and half-orphans would continue to dwindle; 2. to relocate in the country and gradually develop a program to care for more children from broken homes, more children with problems; or 3. to specialize in the care of the severely disturbed, mentally retarded, or delinquent. The approach deemed most desirable by the consultants was the second. "It would recognize the needs for future service and insure the institution a place in child care programs for the future," they said, recommending that the program of care be directed toward older children ages 10 to 18, from broken homes, who could be helped by group care on more of a short-term basis.

Other specific recommendations in the Broten Report were to construct a new facility with six cottages, housing no more than 10 to 15 children per cottage, to hire a full-time caseworker and recreation director, and continue the farm program with modifications including hiring a farm manager.

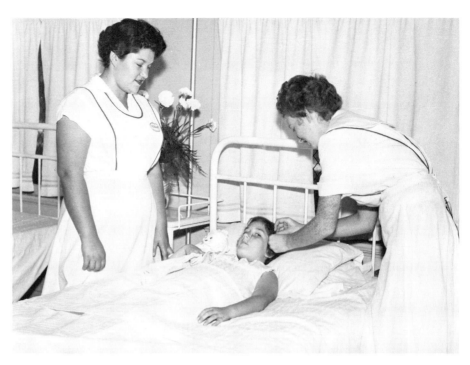
Isolating illnesses in the Infirmary helped avoid family epidemics.

"Childhood years are so important," concluded the report, "and if we can assist children and families to find happiness, we can prevent great misfortune in later years. Times change and the type of services change too. The responsibilities do not grow less. They grow greater and more complicated."[22]

At the time of the study there were 63 children, ages 7 to 21, under the care of Thompson Orphanage. Some had lived on campus for as little as two months, others up to 14 years. The highest percentage of these were classified as orphans or half-orphans, despite national trends to the contrary. One factor which made this figure appear higher was The Duke Endowment designation of 'orphan' as any child whose parents had not made contact for seven years. Once again, Thompson Orphanage appeared to veer away from an established trend. In 1928, superintendent William Wheeler had defended the institution's acceptance of dependent children with living parents while most other institutions were taking in only true orphans or half-orphans. Now that the pendulum had swung in the opposite direction, child-caring institutions accepting almost exclusively children from broken homes, Thompson Orphanage saw its percentage of orphans on the rise. In January, 1953 there were only five true orphans in residence; in September, 1956 there were 15. In contrast, the numbers of children with both parents living declined from 27 in January, 1953 to just seven in September, 1956.[23]

The continued emphasis on farming at Thompson Orphanage was also at odds with a definite opposing trend. It was Red Whisnant's contention that the farm program, in addition to providing milk, meat, and produce for the table, built character and responsibility. He consistently pointed with pride to the youngster's achievements in their 4-H Club, the only 4-H Club in the nation located in the heart of a city. Farming and related homemaking activities kept the youngsters so busy, they rarely had time to watch the first television sets donated to each cottage in 1952.

The Broten Report admitted certain reservations about the farm program, such as the amount of work expected of the children and the profitability of operating both the farm and dairy, but agreed farming "should be an asset" in any continuing program if "the aim is not to make each child into a farmer and make him like the farm."[24]

"A NEW-FANGLED OPERATION"

In 1956, the farm yielded a total of $25,780.93 worth of produce, used either as food for the children or livestock, or sold at a profit of $7,775.71. These figures were presented by Whisnant at a special meeting of the Board of Managers, called June 27, 1957 to consider whether to continue the farm operation in any relocation of the orphanage. He said:

> To me, the real value of your farm is not in the food that we raise that is consumed by the children and livestock, but in the moral uplift and attitude that is instilled in the children by having something to do ... To me, the farm is a vital part of our life ... you must decide to either abandon your farm program or meet the situation and start to build.[25]

Whisnant was anxious to get on with building the modern dairy barns necessary before the herd could be moved from the path of the impending shopping center construction. Whether or not the entire orphanage moved to the country, the cows, which had been tolerated for years by the City against local ordinance, had to go.

The Board responded by authorizing the special planning committee to borrow up to $125,000 to move the dairy operation to Cedarbrook Farm, supporting, in effect, the value of the farm program in any future development.

Most of the farming operation, including hogs, laying hens, beef cattle, horses, mules and tractors, tillers, plows, wagons, hay baler, combine and trucks had already moved to the Cedarbrook property by the end of 1957. Early in the following year, the herd of 35 Jersey cows was evicted from the pastures bordering noisy Independence Boulevard and relocated to a modern dairy on the quiet, country farm, causing "an orphanage official" (doubtless it was the superintendent) to comment, "The cows are the only ones rich enough to afford a new home."[26] Clyde Osborne, rural life editor for *The Charlotte Observer* described the new dairy as "ultramodern . . . one of those new-fangled, push-button operations."[27] There were automatic feeders, hay balers and loaders, and milking machines. "We're happy with our new location," Whisnant was quoted in the article. "We wouldn't think of trading back. The cattle like it here. The hogs like it. And the chickens like it. Everyone is happy."[28]

THE OLD PASTURE GETS A NEW LOOK

The Thompson Orphanage pasture land was slowly transformed into a 250,000-square foot shopping center between May, 1957 and October 28, 1959 when Red Whisnant was invited to take part in the gala opening ceremony for the Charlottetown Mall. Joining with Charlotte Mayor Pro-Tem Herbert Hitch, Whisnant helped bury a time capsule filled with mementos, records and predictions about what life would be like 25 years into the future. Surrounding them, and the crowd of 6,000 people who came to witness the event, was the Southeast's first enclosed shopping mall, with 40 stores ready to do business. There was a festive mood everywhere in the mall, promoted as a 'tropical paradise' and decorated with hundreds of tropical trees, plants, and birds in three-tiered wooden cages. Girls dressed in sarongs strolled the mall giving away baby palm trees, the Colonial Store provided 2,000 free loaves of bread, and

The first day of Charlottetown Mall construction.

Roses' lunch counter advertised a hamburger and milkshake for 39 cents.[29] Outside, flashy DeSotos and two-toned Chevys lined the parking lot which had been made by covering over Sugar Creek. The only competition that morning was an appearance by Fabian at Belk's record bar downtown[30], and perhaps too, a few stubborn memories of less tropical scenes: ragged corn fields, lazy cows, and young orphanage boys perched high atop tractors.

On the day of Charlottetown Mall's grand opening celebration, there were just 58 children living at the nearly adjacent Thompson Orphanage. The number of children under care had continued to decline in the years since the Broten Report, a phenomenon the superintendent attributed to "Social Security, boarding homes and other improvements in our field of welfare"[31] which had reduced the need for institutional care. "The source from which we draw our children continues on the down grade," he said, referring to increased cases of broken homes and resulting emotional problems.[32] He cautioned that the program for the future ought to be carefully considered in view of these changing conditions.

THE HOPKIRK REPORT

In light of these changing trends which had finally caught up to Thompson Orphanage, and the approaching retirement age of the Whisnants, the Board of Managers, through a new committee on future policies and programs,

again commissioned a survey of the orphanage. Howard W. Hopkirk, a nationally-recognized consultant in the field of child care and welfare who was recommended by The Duke Endowment, spent several days in Charlotte, beginning July 22, 1959, visiting the orphanage and farm and also talking with representatives of The Duke Endowment, Board of Education, Welfare Department, United Community Services, Children's Home Society of North Carolina, and the Alexander Home. His report, together with the Broten Report, formed the basis of a new direction for the Thompson Orphanage.

"We have had the benefit of two outside-objective surveys made over a span of three years, explained the committee on future policies, "both of which concur in appraising the need for the services of the orphanage and the program to be followed."[33]

Recommendations from the Hopkirk Report were analyzed by the committee and presented to the Board of Managers on January 29, 1960. Those policies favored by the committee included:

a. Child rehabilitation as the key concept. "Due to changing economic conditions, urbanization, increased longevity of life and other reasons, the basic need which the Orphanage now faces is provision for the care and welfare of children from broken homes."[34] At the time of the survey, 29 of the 58 children under care were from broken homes.

b. Flexibility in the types of services provided, to include institutional or group care, and foster care in boarding homes and small cottages.

c. A shift from child-centered to family-centered goals. " ... Children from broken homes do have a mother and/or father to which they can return if and when the family can be rehabilitated to resume and accept the responsibilities that a family has one to another."[35]

d. Development of a social service department to "control intake, maintain the relations needed with public welfare and church representatives referring children and assisting in their rehabilitation."[36] The survey revealed that very little documentation was preserved in the children's records, but rather, in the heads of the superintendent and his wife. "It may seem morbid," said Hopkirk in his report," but if the Superintendent and Supervising Matron should be killed in the same auto accident, their successors would find that most of the working information on the children under care had disappeared."[37]

e. Hiring an assistant superintendent. "In order to further the proposed change-over from an exclusively institutional service to a more diversified program, the Assistant Superintendent should be experienced in child welfare and with a masters degree in social work."[38]

f. Re-examining the value of the farm operation.

g. Increasing state-wide public relations, particularly as a new program thrust is developed.

h. Construction of an administrative center, and group cottages on the Mecklenburg County farm property.

While embracing these new philosophies, the committee also cautioned against abandoning the purpose of the institution as originally contained in its charter: "to prepare orphans and homeless children for the duties and responsibilities of life." To use the assets of the orphanage, including endowment funds, real estate, and rental income, for any other purposes, said the Board committee, "would constitute a violation of fiduciary responsibilities so long as there is such a need with respect to orphans and homeless children."[39]

The Hopkirk Report expressed confidence in the institution's financial position with regard to implementing the various recommendations. "The institution has fared well in obtaining support needed for its work. It seems reasonable to presume that within a year or two the operating budget as suggested . . . approximately $165,000 could be realized, in addition to any operation of the farm or dairy."[40]

LOSS OF AN ADVOCATE, LEADER, AND FRIEND

For the first time in 37 years, the Board of Managers meeting on January 29, 1960 where results of the Hopkirk survey were presented, was presided over by a new chairman. The Rt. Rev. Richard H. Baker, assumed the office of Bishop of the Diocese of North Carolina, and chairman of the Thompson Orphanage Board of Managers, following the death of Bishop Edwin

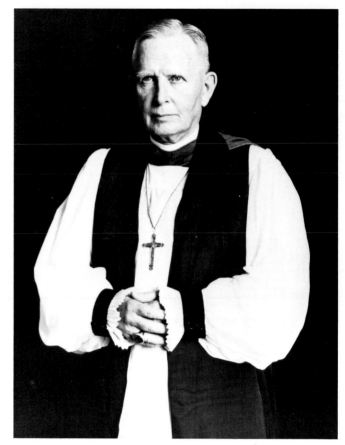

Bishop Edwin A. Penick

A. Penick on April 6, 1959 at the age of 72.

Penick had been a loyal advocate, leader and friend to the Thompson Orphanage since his arrival in Charlotte as rector of St. Peter's Church in August, 1919. When elected Bishop Coadjutor of the Diocese of North Carolina in 1922, he was, at age 35, the youngest member of the House of Bishops. And he maintained both a youthful appearance and outlook, complimented by a boundless good humor, throughout the remainder of his life. A skilled administrator, he led the orphanage through its successful building campaign in 1924 and ably managed its business affairs for over 30 years as chairman of the Board of Managers. At the time of his death, the institution continued to bear the stamp of his influence, most notably in its desire to better serve North Carolina's children in need.

"He was always cheerful, patient and helpful," eulogized his fellow Board members. "He knew many of the children by name, and they all loved him."[41] A memorial included in the minutes of January 29, 1960 meeting affirmed:

Bishop Penick was a man of many talents — he was a scholar and profound student of The Bible; he was an able administrator as

Youngsters climb steps to the administration building.

The week of March 4-10, 1962 was proclaimed by Governor Terry Sanford as "Thompson Orphanage Week" and a state radio hook-up originating at WIST in Charlotte on the evening of Ash Wednesday, featured Bishops Thomas H. Darst of the Diocese of East Carolina, Richard H. Baker of the Diocese of North Carolina, M. George Henry of the Diocese of Western North Carolina, and Thomas A. Fraser, Bishop Coadjutor of the Diocese of North Carolina discussing the role of the Episcopal church and the operation of the orphanage.

The entire front page of *The Charlotte Observer's* Sunday feature section for March 4, 1962 was devoted to the celebration of "Seventy-Five Happy Years."

> Thompson Orphanage, in the heart of Charlotte, will reach a grandfatherly age Wednesday — 75 years. During those 75 years, the orphanage has been mother and father as well as grandfather to the 1,194 children who have passed through its doors.

The public was invited to open house each day between 1-5 p.m. during the birthday celebration.

Aside from its nostalgic look at orphanage life, the article was significant in revealing a marked new emphasis in the institution's child care program:

> The orphanage is working now to rehabilitate children and their families so that the children can return to their own homes. 'We're trying to rehabilitate all the families that we possibly can,' Mrs. Whisnant says. 'The children stay here until their homes are re-established.'

Its future plans also emphasized not only the move to a new physical plant in the country, but a move toward increased family rehabilitation and short-term residential care.

shown in the conduct of the affairs of the Diocese and its institutions; he was one of the most skilled and fair Parliamentarians to ever preside over a Diocesan Convention or Board; he was a brilliant preacher, heard throughout the Church; he was active in the affairs of The National Church — serving as a member of The National Council; and when he died was the senior active Bishop of The House of Bishops, — he helped to organize and was President of The North Carolina Council of Churches; he organized The Laymens Association of The Diocese and established Vade Mecum Camps and Conferences, besides organizing The Young Peoples Service League of the Diocese.[42]

"SEVENTY-FIVE HAPPY YEARS"

Continuing to carve out its appropriate role from among the many recommendations and observations made in the Broten and Hopkirk reports, the Thompson Orphanage entered its seventy-fifth year of service. The institution used the occasion of its 1962 anniversary celebration to spotlight past and present accomplishments, and as a springboard for disclosing its future plans.

STAFF POSITIONS ADDED

An assistant superintendent was hired just prior to the seventy-fifth anniversary celebration to help carry out these new goals. Robert Dale Noble was the first to hold that title since A.S. Bynum served as assistant superintendent and business manager between 1929 and 1939. An Episcopalian raised in Charlotte, Robert Noble was familiar with the operation of the orphanage and met the educational requirements as suggested by the Hopkirk study, holding a masters degree in social work from the University of North Carolina. Prior to his appointment as assistant superintendent, Noble was executive secretary to the Community Chest in Anderson, S.C., campaign director of the United Appeal and staff associate of the Social Planning Council in Charlotte.

In October, 1962 the orphanage hired its first permanent, trained director of social services to take on the challenges of its new commitment to child and family rehabilitation. Mrs. Mary Wunder, who began her career in social work 25 years earlier, traveling the Kentucky mountains on horseback to reach her clients, came to Thompson Orphanage from the domestic relations court in Winston-Salem where she had been chief probation officer. Her training for the position also included a masters degree from the

Mary Wunder

Celebrating Thompson's 75th Anniversary in March, 1962: (left to right) Bishop M. George Henry, Bishop Richard Baker, the Rev. William H. Wheeler, M.D. Whisnant, Pearl Whisnant, and Bishop Thomas A. Fraser.

School of Social Work at the University of North Carolina.

FOSTER HOMES

Other elements adopted from the Broten and Hopkirk reports quickly began to appear in the Thompson Orphanage program. In January, 1963, Mary Wunder noted that the orphanage had obtained a license from the State Department of Public Welfare to begin a foster home placement program, making it only the third church-related institution in the state to expand its child caring services into private homes. The new venture was called the Thompson Orphanage Family Care Program. By May, 1963, five children had been placed in three foster homes in Charlotte, Spray, and Winston-Salem. The orphanage adopted a policy of accepting applications to become foster homes only from Episcopal families, in the belief that the church would remain a strong influence in the development of the new Family Care Program.

"I was a little scared knowing that I had agreed to take care of three small pre-school children," said a foster parent in Spray, N.C. "But when I saw them at my door, I knew right away that everything was going to be all right."[43] Since pre-school children were too young to be accepted for group care at the orphanage, the foster home program enabled the institution to greatly extend its services.

GROUP HOME

Plans for the first group home began with a study committee appointed in 1962 by Thomas H. Wright, Bishop of the Diocese of East Carolina, and headed by James C. Fox of Wilmington. Other members were Ed Borden, Charles Norwood, Jr., Sefton Abbott and George Vann. After considering six different locations, the committee settled in 1964 on Goldsboro as the site of the state's first group home, primarily because of its location within the Diocese of East Carolina where it could serve children without removing them so far from their community setting, and its abundance of resources such as recreation, medical, and education services. Land was provided at a greatly reduced cost and St. Stephen's Church of Goldsboro pledged $2,500 in its upcoming budget for oper-

ation of the home. A groundbreaking ceremony was held on Sunday, November 1, 1964, led by Bishop Thomas H. Wright.

Located in a residential section of the city, the home was designed for up to 12 children and their 'parents,' a couple who would live at the facility and create a situation as similar to a real family as possible. Advantages of the group home, as explained by Robert Noble, were the ability to keep children from the same family together, and to care for them not far from their original homes. "Our emphasis is on rehabilitation of the family," said Noble at the groundbreaking ceremony. "With institutional care in Charlotte, it becomes rather difficult to talk realistically about working with a family that lives in Goldsboro or New Bern."[44]

A large portion of the funds to assist in the new orphanage projects continued to come from bequests and private contributions. During 1962 Robert Noble made a concerted public relations effort to reach clergy and laymen across the state with a more factual picture of the institution's financial status, its changing emphasis in child welfare, and the need for additional services. The Thanksgiving appeal was made directly into the homes of Episcopal church members, increasing the giving by over $3,000 compared to the previous year. The momentum of giving slacked off during 1963, due in part to the state's shaky farm economy, a competition for funds within the church for a Home for the Aging, and "a general belief that Thompson Orphanage is wealthy."[45]

In addition to canvassing the state for increased financial support, Robert Noble spent countless hours with the Whisnants, absorbing from them vital bits of information about the children, and about running an orphanage. "I have gained a completely new respect for the work of our Superintendent," he told the Board of Managers.[46]

> When I came a year ago, I believe that I had a healthy respect for the work of a Superintendent of an institution; however, my idea of the Superintendent was that of mostly administrator ... I have found out since I have been here that the Whisnants far from being just administrators have had to be caseworkers, plumbers, recreation workers, nurses, house parents, cooks, firemen, farmer, and handy man, to name just a few.[47]

Noble was particularly observant of the role, since the Whisnants announced in July, 1964 their plans to retire the following year.

DIOCESAN INSTITUTIONAL STUDY

In the early months of 1963, the Executive Council of the Diocese of North Carolina instructed the Diocesan Department of Institutions to study the programs of all institutions receiving financial support from the diocese. This study was completed in November, 1964 and presented at the January 25, 1965 meeting of the Thompson Orphanage Board of Managers. In it were various suggestions relating to administration of the institution, including more frequent meetings of the Board and Executive Committee, and appointment of a consultant from the Group Child Care Project "to aid the Board of Managers, the Executive Committee, and the staff of the institution in moving into a sound program of group care." That consultant, Dr. Alan Keith-Lucas, had already been retained in 1964 to help interpret and implement the Hopkirk Report.

One of the final recommendations was for "careful consideration to the development of a program that shall include Negro children," an action long supported by Bishop Edwin Penick for all church institutions. The suggestion came on the heels of a significant meeting held in April, 1964 in Washington, D.C., co-sponsored by the Children's Bureau of the Department of Health, Education and Welfare, the Child Welfare League of America, National Council of the Episcopal Church, Methodist Board of Hospitals and Homes, National Conference of Catholic Charities, and the National Lutheran Council. At that meeting, representatives took the first steps toward achieving racial integration in child-caring institutions. In response, the Board of Managers of Thompson Orphanage, meeting May 29, 1964, passed a resolution stating:

> The Admission Policy of the Thompson Orphanage contains no reference to race, color, or creed. The final factor determining the admission of the child and whether service is provided through group care, or the use of foster homes, is what will be best for the individual child in view of all the factors involved in his particular situation.

Symptoms of racial awareness seemed to be everywhere. The eyes of the nation turned to Charlotte in 1965 as Judge James McMillan ordered the county's schools to use cross-town busing to achieve integration. "Amos & Andy" was withdrawn from television syndication after protests against its stereotyped characters. There was an undercurrent of restlessness across the country, vented in civil rights demonstrations and rallies against the war in Vietnam, in popular songs like "I Can't Get No Satisfaction," and even in art, the most memorable offering of the year being Andy Warhol's painting of a giant Campbell's Tomato Soup can.

Like the hordes of young people in search of themselves, the Thompson Orphanage was seeking out a new direction for itself in the face of evident and predicted trends, a direction which didn't seem to fit anymore with Pop's old farm hat or Mom's idyllic picnics. While searching for clues to a new identity in the traditions of the past, the Whisnants found the future had overtaken them from behind.

Manley Dowell Whisnant and his wife officially retired on June 30, 1965, and with them went a large chunk of Thompson Orphanage history. They withdrew to a quiet life along the Pamlico Sound at Belhaven, N.C., contenting themselves with scrapbook memories, letters and visits from orphanage children, and annual pilgrimages to Charlotte for alumni reunions.

In their 25 years at the institution, the Whisnants had formed a multitude into a family, giving over 800 children their roots in a unique heritage. Journalist Hodding Carter described the phenomenon best:

> There are only two bequests we can hope to give our children. One of these is roots; the other, wings.

FOOTNOTES

1. Emily Whitehurst Stone, "The Ties That Bind," *The Charlotte Observer,* September 29, 1985, p. 7F.

2. "Annual Report," January, 1957, p. 1.

3. Edwin A. Penick to M.D. Whisnant, August 28, 1956, Thompson Orphanage Historical Files, Charlotte, N.C.

4. "Annual Report," January, 1957, p. 1.

5. "Annual Report," January, 1958, p. 1.

6. "Report of Special Planning Committee," May, 1957, p. 3, Thompson Orphanage Historical Files, Charlotte, N.C.

7. "Pierson Report," September 20, 1956, Thompson Orphanage Historical Files, Charlotte, N.C.

8. "The Group Child Care Project — Confidential Report to the Superintendent and the Board of Managers," April 16, 1957, p. 6.

9. Ibid., p. 7.

10. Ibid., p. 45.

11. Ibid.

12. Ibid., pp. 8-9.

13. Ibid., p. 11.

14. Ibid., p. 12.

15. Ibid., pp. 12-13.

16. Ibid., pp. 13-14.

17. Ibid., p. 15.

18. Ibid.

19. Ibid., p. 16.

20. Ibid., p. 17.

21. Ibid., p. 20.

22. Ibid., p. 1.

23. Ibid., p. 4.

24. Ibid., pp. 36-37.

25. "Superintendent's Report To Special Meeting Of The Board Of Managers," June 27, 1957, p. 2.

26. Porter Munn, "Remember Queen City Cow Herd?" *The Charlotte Observer,* October 28, 1959, p. 21C.

27. Clyde Osborne, "Theirs Is Push-Button Farm," *The Charlotte Observer,* November 2, 1959, p. 4B.

28. Ibid.

29. "Fanfare Opens Charlottetown Mall Today," *The Charlotte Observer,* October 28, 1959, p. 2C.

30. "Mall Opening To Be Today," *The Charlotte Observer,* October 28, 1959, p. 1B.

31. "Annual Report," January, 1959, p. 1.

32. Ibid.

33. "Report of the Committee Appointed to Study and Recommend to the Board of Managers the Future Policies and Program of the Thompson Orphanage and Training Institution," January 29, 1960, p. 2.

34. Ibid.

35. "Recent Developments at Thompson Orphanage," *The Mission Herald,* May, 1962, p. 6.

36. "Report of the Committee on Future Policies," p. 5.

37. Howard Hopkirk, "Report of Survey," January 18, 1960, p. 24.

38. Ibid.

39. Ibid., p. 6.

40. Ibid., p. 15.

41. "In Memoriam," January 29, 1960, p. 2, Thompson Orphanage Historical Files, Charlotte, N.C.

42. Ibid., p. 1.

43. *Thompson Orphanage Alumni Association Newsletter,* June 9, 1963, p. 6.

44. Frank Warren, "A New Concept In Care For Homeless," *Goldsboro News-Argus,* November 1, 1964, p. 8.

45. "Report of the Assistant Superintendent to the Board of Managers," January 31, 1964, p. 1.

46. "Report of the Assistant Superintendent," January 25, 1963, p. 1.

47. Ibid.

Chapter 8

Growing Pains

1966 — 1969

In June, 1965, Robert D. Noble became superintendent of a residential home for children caught up in the center of a city's burgeoning growth. Thompson Orphanage was crowded in from every side by urban redevelopment, threatened by changing street patterns and traffic congestion, and wary of rising crime. There was an uneasiness in the air during the latter years of the 1960's, fed by the general disquiet of the times, and an urgency to put into practice the institution's most recently defined goals.

LOOKING TO THE FUTURE

In his first report to the Board as superintendent, Noble detailed his outlook on the future of Thompson Orphanage, showing how it "might serve the needs of children and families in a world and in a time when change and uncertainty are paramount."[1] Without discounting the "rich heritage" of its past, Thompson Orphanage he said, "must concentrate on the future . . . What we do now with our energies and what we do now with this tremendous resource imbodied [sic] in the structure and organization called Thompson Orphanage, is all important."[2]

He described the changing nature of children and families being served by the institution:

> Most of our children come to us from broken homes; homes which have experienced divorces, separations, desertions, mental illness and many other unpleasant and devastating situations. When children came to us years ago as orphans . . . chances are that they did come from a fine family . . . had strong, sound foundations on which to build their new life at Thompson Orphanage. The nature of the children coming to us now, though, is quite different. They have homes; they have mothers and fathers whom they love in spite of all the tragic things that have gone before. They want to be back home no matter what the situation is there, and most of all they are not at all grateful for Thompson Orphanage. They resent being here; they resent all the things which seem to separate them from their families. And . . . their families are not grateful either . . . Often times these families come to us—not of their own choosing—but at the direction of the Welfare Department and the Domestic Relations Court.[3]

To adequately deal with these new pressures, Noble stressed the importance of hiring additional, professionally-trained staff members, such as Bill Brittain, director of the newly-created Division of Group Child Care who was responsible for the overall campus program. "We are discovering that the housemothers who have so ably served us in the past are no longer equal to the present day's task," Noble observed.[4] He suggested hiring younger women who "in addition to dedication and love for children" possessed "personal security, understanding, and ability."[5] For these qualities, he said, the institution must pay a higher salary than the current top wages of $2,100 a year plus board.

To accommodate more children on campus, the cottages, though still divided by sex, were changed to include children of differing age groups. "With the support of our cottage mothers," reported Noble, "we launched into this new venture as if we had good sense, and we increased our population by a third in less than two months time . . . Nevertheless, it has been a long hot summer and all of us are glad to see school again."[6]

In the area of ultimate support for its new programs, the new superintendent was realistic: "There is no getting around the fact that the costs of the quality care necessary to meet today's needs will be great. Even Howard Hopkirk's estimate of $165,000 several years ago is low."[7] Noble suggested a number of alternatives including increased public relations within the church, broadening the institution's base of support, and stimulating growth of the Endowment Fund.

He envisioned Thompson Orphanage in a precarious balance between the traditions of the past, and the demands of the future:

> . . . We must be willing to throw off the yoke of tradition and become flexible to the need, always though, maintaining the high standards set by our traditions . . . Thompson Orphanage is at the brink. It can follow along after the field of child care, or it can be a part of the growth of this field."[8]

GOODBYE "DADDY GRACE"

Noble's lofty goals for the institution were complicated by its physical location in the center city. Brooklyn, for years the orphanage's closest neighbor, was already gone. Sledgehammers had leveled the first house in the designated urban renewal project in 1961. The wood and tar-paper shacks, dirt streets, and open sewers had been replaced with the beginnings of Charlotte's governmental plaza which would include the Law Enforcement Center, Education Center, an overhead walkway, and the familiar fountain of Marshall Park, plopped almost directly on the site of a home once occupied by orphanage superintendent Walter J. Smith, and which most recently had held "Daddy Grace's" United House of Prayer for All People. "Oh, I can remember walking up to McDowell Street to watch those splendid 'Daddy Grace' parades," said former orphanage resident Mary Froebe. "We were the only white folks there!" McDowell Street, at one time called the murder capital of America, had been stripped of its decaying buildings and was becoming a quiet paved avenue leading to Morehead Street. The City of Charlotte had proposed an extension of Third Street which threatened to cut in half the remaining ten acres of the Thompson Orphanage before it linked with Providence Road on the other side of Independence Boulevard and had its eye on a slice of the campus for widening Fourth Street.

In the shadow of uptown Charlotte's rising skyline, the 80-year old orphanage was showing its age. "The plumber is on our campus so frequently that one would think he is a member of our staff," observed Robert Noble in 1966.[9] A crack in the 70-foot boiler house chimney, erected in 1925, had to be repaired in 1966 and the capacity of the boilers increased to supply sufficient heat. During the previous winter, Kenan Cottage had gone without heat for six weeks. The properties committee reported in May, 1966, "It is becoming increasingly difficult to maintain the buildings and equipment on this campus in a usable condition." The only substantial luxuries added during maintenance and repairs to the buildings were hot water heaters for each cottage, to replace old woodburning stoves used to heat water, and washers and dryers so that the girls no longer had to spend their afternoons in the central laundry.

The large brick cottages, though drafty and insufficiently heated, were amazingly clean. In

The administration building stands sentry over an ageing campus.

his report to the Board of Managers in January, 1967, Bill Brittain, director of Group Child Care, admitted:

> The Health Department inspector recently said he could give us a B grade every time on our poor facilities alone but he gives us an A because he is amazed at how clean most of the cottages are kept. Some of these women are breaking their backs trying to keep these old buildings clean. I, too, am amazed at how they do it as most cottages don't even have a vacuum cleaner.[10]

LIFE AT THE OLD "T.O."

The children did their part to help the old "T.O." as they affectionately called it, planting grass and flowers in all the yards, painting and redecorating the library. The boys cleaned out the old gymnasium and by early 1966 the thud of bouncing basketballs and volleyballs could again be heard on campus. Soon a basketball team was organized to play against local church teams.

The hub of campus activities and recreation shifted back to the Fourth Street campus following the cut-backs in the farming operation after Red Whisnant retired. The dairy herd was sold for $11,000 at the end of 1965 to Godley Brothers of Charlotte and most of the remaining farm equipment sold at auction.[11] The number of farm hands was reduced from three to one farm manager. "Thompson Orphanage is out of farming as a business operation," explained Robert Noble in his 'Report on the Future.' "We now have a beef herd, only enough hogs for our own use, and a vegetable garden."[12]

More emphasis began to be placed on bringing new resources to the campus and involving the children more fully in community activities. A cadre of community volunteers offered their skills, teaching piano, body-building, and arts and crafts. Members of the Women's Cooperative Guild provided transportation for the children's medical and dental appointments and other activities. Volunteers from Queens College and St. Martin's Church worked as tutors for some of the younger students. Thompson Orphanage guilds from all three Episcopal dioceses in the state joined together as sponsors of individual cottages, providing money for clothing, Christmas gifts and other needs. It was a mutually satisfying relationship for the children, and their sponsors who kept up with each child's needs and interests. A letter to the sponsors of Kenan Cottage for girls in 1966 was filled with news as well as gratitude for their support.

> Enclosed you will find a picture of your cottage, including the girls who now reside there. I hope that you can pass the picture around . . . so that all the ladies may have the opportunity to see what a nice looking group of girls they support. The Kenan girls have been very busy lately. We have formed a teenage youth group. They have as their project 'Making Thompson A Better Place In Which To Live.' Bobbie is presently enrolled in a Nurse's Aide course and will graduate the 26th of April . . . Peggy and Maria are seniors this year and will graduate June 7. Peggy plans to continue her education by attending Business School. Maria has marriage on her mind and plans to seek employment in the Charlotte area. Sally C. is a very active high school Sophomore. She is a cheerleader at Garinger High School and is very active in extracurricular activities. She has completed her drivers' education course, has her permit for thirty days and today will try for her drivers' license. Is she excited — and a little nervous, I might add. Ann and Thresa are both honor students at Piedmont Jr. High . . . Lupie, Becky, Robbie Jo, Janice, Joyce and Sally Q. are typical teenagers. They are mighty particular with their dress, especially when the opposite sex is around! . . . It is now time to purchase spring and summer clothing. During the next few weeks we will make many trips down town to get new Easter outfits. I hope you ladies will support the girls in Kenan as well as you did with your Christmas gifts . . . Without your valuable support we could not offer our children many of the opportunities they now have. Bill Brittain.[13]

All of the youngster's activities pointed to a changing, more expansive attitude about institutional child care. The children joined local Boy Scout and Girl Scout troops, the YMCA and YWCA, and various school teams and clubs. Some of the girls volunteered as candy stripers for local hospitals and many of the boys took up golf, perhaps wishing for that golf course proposed for the orphanage property back in 1929. Teenagers were encouraged to bring their dates and friends to the campus for dances and students were allowed to take off-

Volunteer tutors helped youngsters improve school performance.

campus jobs after school.

Summers became especially busy with trips and events sponsored by community groups and businesses. The children were treated to beach weekends and deep-sea fishing excursions, picnics and boat rides on the Catawba River, and baseball games in Atlanta to watch the former Milwaukee Braves. Each child had at least a two-week vacation off campus, either with relatives or at scout and church camps including Vade Mecum, Henry, Thunderbird, and Leach. Often the children went by truckloads out to the farm property to pick beans, corn or okra, the reward for filling a basket being a swim in the lake or a juicy watermelon.

The emphasis on community involvement was made more difficult by the institution's inhospitable neighborhood. No youngsters, including teens, were allowed to leave campus after dark except by car, nor were they allowed to walk to the bus stop. Unlike earlier years, activities were no longer within walking dis-

tance. Schools, and after-school programs, were far from campus. The problem was compounded in September, 1966 when, in anticipation of the move to Margaret Wallace Road, students were re-assigned to Albemarle Road Junior High and Independence High School, forcing the orphanage to buy its own bus.

GOLDSBORO HOME OPENS

While augmenting its residence program in Charlotte, Thompson Orphanage continued to expand its services in foster home and group care. The group cottage in Goldsboro, under construction since August, 1965, was opened on February 5, 1966 when Mary Wunder, director of the Division of Planning with Families and Children, arrived in snow and mud with five children, and not a blanket to sleep under. By the following year there were plenty of blankets, and 12 children living in the home, in addition to 62 on the Charlotte campus and 9 in foster care. The group home was built with funds accumulated from lease of the Charlottetown Mall property.

To better describe its work as a multi-service agency providing family-centered programs, the institution changed its name in September, 1965, to 'Episcopal Child Care Services of North Carolina, of the Thompson Orphanage and Training Institution.' While it used the shortened version, 'Episcopal Child Care Services,' the institution continued, by habit, to be known and referred to as 'Thompson Orphanage.'

STATISTICS BECOME PEOPLE

The name change signaled a new emphasis in care, but it did not mean that orphans had suddenly disappeared. Many true orphans and half-orphans remained in the program after 1965, and others continued to be admitted along with children from troubled homes. Over half of all the children in care by the Fall of 1967 were orphans or half-orphans, "illustrating," said Mary Wunder, "that while we talk of broken homes, we still have to face the fact that many children are deprived of parental care by reason of death."[14] Yet, even in the case of full orphans, there was almost always some relative actively involved in the child's plan of care, a direct departure from previous years when the institution made no attempt to contact or involve childrens' families. As a result, there was also a marked increase in monetary support from parents and relatives. "It is not only a help money wise," reported Mary Wunder, "but represents our complete philosophy of continually keeping parents and relatives involved."[15]

The causes of broken homes, aside from the death of parents, continued to mount, as did applications for admission to Thompson Orphanage programs. More common reasons for admission became divorce, abuse, mental illness, alcoholism, and neglect. In December, 1966 the institution admitted for residential care a 15-year old girl and a 12-year old boy, "so quiet and nice looking," described Mary Wunder to the Board, that "one would never know that they have been witness to murder, they have been objects of incest, they have lived in the home of an alcoholic mother and a criminal father, and can never remember a time when

Festivities mark dedication of Goldsboro Group Home.

there was any peace or happiness."[16] The statistics of previous studies had turned into people; people who needed the increasingly specialized care offered by Episcopal Child Care Services.

MAKING THE BEST OF AN "ABNORMAL SITUATION"

The children accepted into the campus program brought with them a challenging new set of problems. There were more incidents of running away, aggression, and difficulties in school. Working with children from increasingly troubled family situations placed greater demands on the staff and required a unique breed of people willing to serve as housemothers and cottage parents. Among those were Wayne and Judy Morris, who moved into an old brick cottage on the Thompson Orphanage campus in November, 1968, and instantly increased their family of children from two to twelve. They were the first set of houseparents for a new family cottage which took children out of sexually segregated cottages and placed them in a more normal living situation.

Imagine: One large old house, a young married couple, a dozen children and almost as many synchronized radios vibrating with the voice of Jose Feliciano singing 'C'mon baby, light my fire.' That's a typical late afternoon scene for Judy and Wayne Morris who began a new chapter in their lives one day last November when they moved into a newly set up family cottage at Thompson Orphanage . . . The pair of 26-year olds are mature enough to serve as parents to the group of 10 to 17-year-olds and youthful enough to be their friends. . . . The Morrises try to treat all the children as if they were their own — even to the point of setting the curfew earlier than in some of the other cottages . . . It's a 24-hour job full of details familiar to all parents, things like checking clothing, making sure hair is neatly combed and beds made, administering cough medicine in the middle of the night . . . Being cot-

A battle takes shape in front of St. Mary's Chapel and Stedman Cottage.

tage parents means, 'That's exactly what we are — parents to them ... Dates have to meet us, talk with us and get scared of us just like in a normal home. These kids have problems other kids don't have,' said Wayne. 'It's an abnormal situation for them to grow up in but they're really no different from other children. I think they're more realistic.'[17]

Though they filled the role of surrogate parents, the Morrises weren't allowed to be called 'Mom' and 'Dad'; the orphanage insisted that they be 'Mr. and Mrs. Morris.'

During the late 1960's, Thompson Orphanage remained in a state of transition, not only tailoring its services to meet new demands, but trying to maintain its physically crumbling campus while building a new one. There were constant cutbacks in service at the present location as the orphanage faced proposed building cost estimates of $1 million or more for a new campus. In 1967, the annual Thanksgiving Offering amounted to only 20 per cent of the institution's income, contrasted with 1947 when church giving furnished over 50 per cent of the budget. "Many people, including some clergy, are under the mistaken impression that the Home is well financed," observed Executive Committee member the Rev. David Woodruff in 1967.[18]

Episcopal Churchwomen from all three dioceses took up the challenge in 1968, raising more than $15,000 for the orphanage through cake sales, fairs, bazaars, dances, clothing sales, proceeds from gift shops and other ventures. Their efforts spilled over into the 1968 Thanksgiving Offering, "the best ever recorded, exceeding all expectations at $41,300."[19]

BUILDING PLANS ANNOUNCED

Plans for the institution's new campus were released in January, 1969 after three years of study and preparation by the special planning committee of the Board of Managers. The 40-acre site at Cedarbrook Farm had been approved by the Board in May, 1966 as the location for the new facility, but decisions on zoning regulations, access roads, architectural plans and other details delayed the start of construction until the beginning of 1969.

The new campus plan included four cottages designed to house a maximum of 12 children each, an activities building with an outdoor swimming pool, administration building, and a residence for the campus director. Moving out into the country, the orphanage also had to build its own roads, water system, sewage system and treatment plant. The cottages were to be clustered around a wooded, central playground and house both boys and girls of differing ages. There was to be no central dining hall; each cottage would have its own kitchen and dining area. The plan also called for construction of a fifth cottage when funds became available.

Architects for the project were Connelly, Winecoff and Tooley Associates, and general contractor, C.P. Street Construction Company.

Building costs were estimated at $1 million, to be financed by $700,000 from unrestricted endowment funds and the remainder from accumulated rentals on the Charlottetown Mall. And while it appeared that the institution could meet the costs of construction, day-to-day operating expenses continued to be a concern. Along with announcement of the institution's building plans Robert Noble added the caution, "It looks as if we're rich, but we're not. We've got to move from our present location for a lot of reasons — it's an unfit place to rear the children, maintenance costs on the old buildings have shot up sky-high, and it's costing us about 10 per cent more every year just to hold the present level of operation."[20]

The disposition of the present 10-acre campus remained uncertain although the City of Charlotte announced its plans to extend Third Street through its center, and to widen Fourth Street. The western edge of the orphanage property also appeared a likely site for part of a new expressway.

"IT'S BEEN A LONG, LONG HAUL"

On the last day of January, 1969, the sun shone for the first time in a week, warming the fields at Cedarbrook Farm where a large crowd gathered for the official groundbreaking ceremony. Over one hundred prominent Episcopal clergy and laymen were present for the special service, written for the occasion by the liturgical commission of the Diocese of North Carolina. Bishop M. George Henry of the Diocese of Western North Carolina opened the ceremony with prayer and Bishop Thomas A. Fraser of the

Diocese of North Carolina turned the first shovelful of dirt.

Others who took their turn with the spade included the Rt. Rev. Moultrie Moore, Jr., Suffragan Bishop of the Diocese of North Carolina, the Rev. W. David Woodruff, chairman of the Executive Committee and rector of St. Andrew's Church in Charlotte, James O. Moore, chairman of the policy committee, Mary Wunder, director of Planning with Families and Children, B.E. Rogers, group child care director, executive director Robert Noble, and four orphanage children each representing their cottages: Cathy Collins, Sidney Cruse, James Threatt, and Rachel Wallace.

As Robert Noble took his turn at scooping up the softened earth, he expressed both relief and anticipation: "This is a grand day, but it's been a long, long haul."[21]

Her coat waving behind her like a kite, nine-year old Rachel Wallace raced with her friends toward the line of waiting cars. The Episcopal church members who had picked her up at school for the groundbreaking service had also promised hamburgers for lunch, and she didn't want to miss out on the treat.

Robert Noble, the Bishops and other invited guests wandered more sedately across the farm land, gesturing and nodding as they envisioned completed buildings, here among a cedar grove, or there beyond the dense tangle of wisteria vines. By year's end the orphanage expected to be in its new home.

The superintendent led the way back to the small rise where cars were parked, inviting everyone back to Fourth Street for a luncheon in the dining hall. As the cars edged slowly off the grass, a caravan of construction vehicles was already threading its way across the meadow. Shirt-sleeved drivers waved heartily. The weather was mild, the afternoon bright. It was a good day to begin.

Rachel Wallace breaks ground for the new Thompson campus, February 1, 1969.

FOOTNOTES

1. Robert Noble, "Report On The Future," January 1966, p. 1.

2. Ibid.

3. Ibid., p. 2.

4. Ibid.

5. Ibid., p. 3.

6. Ibid., p. 5.

7. Ibid., p. 6

8. Ibid., pp. 5, 7.

9. Robert Noble, "Report to the Board," May 27, 1966.

10. "Report of the Director of Group Child Care," January 30, 1967, p. 1.

11. "Report of the Properties Committee," September 17, 1965.

12. Robert Noble, "Report On The Future," p. 4.

13. Bill Brittain, Sponsor's Program Letter, March 26, 1966, Thompson Orphanage Historical Files, Charlotte, N.C.

14. Mary Wunder, "Report to the Board of Managers — Division of Planning with Families and Children," October, 1967.

15. Mary Wunder, "Report to the Board," September 30, 1966.

16. Mary Wunder, "Report to the Board," January 30, 1967.

17. Carole Gray, "Houseparents Dispense Love With Discipline," *The Charlotte News,* April 12, 1969, p. 14A.

18. David Woodruff, "Woodruff Issues Report on Thompson Orphanage Affairs," *The North Carolina Churchman,* October, 1967, p. 16.

19. "Inspired Churchwomen Respond To Child Care Financial Crisis," *Talk 'N Tattle,* Winter, 1969, p. 2.

20. Rita Simpson, "Orphanage Work Slated To Begin," *The Charlotte News,* January 22, 1969, p. 2A.

21. Mamie Zillman, "Man, Nature Bless New Orphanage Site," *The Charlotte Observer,* February 1, 1969, p. 1B.

Chapter 9

Where Have All The Orphans Gone?

1970 — 1979

"The grass is thick with violets, in the dooryard of St. Mary's. For the first time in the chapel's long life, there are no young feet running, taking their toll of spring growth. The Thompson Orphanage has moved away and left St. Mary's in its downtown wildwood. Ivy clings to the mortar between dark bricks, climbing, tangling with budding wild grape vines. The shrubs belong to the redbirds. Fourth Street traffic is muffled, and distant, and the only near sounds are the birds, and the creaking of empty swings in the wind."[1]

Episcopal Child Care Services' new campus came as a Christmas gift to the children who left the 83-year old orphanage for the holidays in December, 1969, returning at the start of the new year not to Fourth Street but to the new facility eight miles to the east, just off Margaret Wallace Road. There were 48 children who made the move, the maximum who could be accommodated in the new cottages. They brought with them expectations of improved living conditions and memories of a past physically left behind.

Staff members did all the initial moving themselves in rented and borrowed trucks, though it took several months to completely clear out the old buildings and get established in the new. The youngsters helped too, often returning to Fourth Street in the afternoons or on weekends to retrieve lingering bits of history.

"MAKE A JOYFUL NOISE"

The new campus was officially dedicated on May 16, 1970 as 'Thompson Childrens' Home,' descriptive not only of the service but of a feeling in the heart.

The children had spent weeks preparing for the dedication day ceremonies, working closely with the 'Homewarming Committee' headed by Mrs. Ann Elliott of the Executive Committee. They made colorful banners proclaiming "Joy-Harmony-Peace" and "Jesus Cares," issued hundreds of invitations to friends across the state to join them in "making a joyful noise" during the celebration, picked and arranged bowls full of flowers, inflated hundreds of balloons, and helped design a poster announcing the event:

Where have all the orphans gone?

For many years, we have dreamed of a new place for our children. A sun-filled place where fresh air is plentiful ... a large and laughing place where young legs can race the wind ... a place to stimulate young minds and encourage young spirits. A place over-flowing with love. The dream is now a reality, and we wish to share our joy with you.[2]

All the girls had their hair styled free for the dedication, compliments of Warner's Hair Styling Studios, The Anthony's, Jack's Beauty Salon and Metrolina Beauty Salon, all in Charlotte. And the boys sported new haircuts too. Everyone was anxious to look his best. It was to be "the children's day" said Ann Elliott.[3]

The festivities began with an open house on Friday, May 15, so the children could show off their new 8,000-square foot cottages. Proudly, they led visitors into every bedroom, bath and kitchen, chattering about family routines and showing off treasured possessions.

'Come and see our bathroom,' said a young man of about 7 named Willy. Willy went in first and looked around and decided, 'Maybe you'd better wait a few minutes.' The guests waited a few minutes while Willy straightened up.

Another fellow confided, 'We don't always keep this clean.'[4]

The cottages were air-conditioned and so attractively furnished that Ann Elliott worried, "We've been awfully afraid that people would think we've been extravagant. We haven't. We've bought things that we know will last, and we've gotten a lot of breaks on the prices."[5] Each of the four brick cottages had six bedrooms, a living room, kitchen, family room and large recreation room. "You couldn't appreciate the new ones unless you had known the old ones," observed executive director Robert Noble.[6]

Episcopal clergy and church members from across the state, friends, family, orphanage alumni and civic leaders from Charlotte joined in the day-long dedication on Saturday, May 16, 1970. Five Bishops, representing all three North Carolina dioceses, led the service: Thomas A. Fraser, Bishop of the Diocese of North Carolina; Thomas H. Wright, Bishop of the Diocese of East Carolina; M. George Henry, Bishop of the Diocese of Western North Carolina; Hunley Elebash, Bishop Coadjutor of the Diocese of

Dedication of Thompson Children's Home, May 16, 1970.

East Carolina; and Moultrie Moore, Jr., Suffragan Bishop of the Diocese of North Carolina. The children held their banners high as they led a procession to each new campus building. At the sound of a trumpet blast, each building received its official blessing from the Bishops.

The last building to be blessed was the administrative center where the crowd unfurled to enjoy a picnic of barbecue, coleslaw and plenty of pies, baked by women of the nine area Episcopal churches. The "joyful noise" continued with music provided by small groups of folk singers accompanied by guitars, and the brass choir of South Mecklenburg High School.

Among the guests were Edwin Clarkson and his cousin Mrs. James P. Caldwell, grandchildren of founding superintendent Edwin Osborne, several relatives of William Wheeler, former superintendent and chaplain who died in 1964, and 'Mom' and 'Pop' Whisnant. William Oates, who came to the orphanage in 1897 and held title to 'the oldest living alumni' was there too.

We had to chop wood for the fire, and milk the cows and pick cotton,' he said. He allowed if he could, he'd come back and be an 'orphan' again, under the present conditions of comfort.[7]

OLD BUILDINGS LEVELED

Almost as quickly as the orphanage moved out, road department crews moved in to stake out the old campus, marking with flags the buildings to be bulldozed for the Third Street extension and diversion of Sugar Creek. Maintenance engineer and houseparent Donald Honeycutt returned to the old Home in June, 1970, to retrieve building cornerstones, plaques, markers and other treasurers. Among his finds was the hollow cornerstone of Smith Cottage, stuffed with the decaying books and papers laid there by Walter Smith in 1912. The Bible and Episcopal Prayer Book were gnawed, the *Charlotte Daily Observer* newspaper in crumbs. An edition of the *Carolina Churchman* containing a history of the orphanage had fared only slightly better. These frayed bits of history, gingerly laid in a box and stored in a basement file drawer in the new administration building, were a poignant reminder of what had been left behind.

By mid-July, 1970, bulldozers were cutting a swath across the old property taking with them the cottages that stood in the path of the Third Street extension: first Kenan, Williamson and Smith, then Christ Church and Baker. When the dust settled on July 11, 1970, only St. Mary's Chapel, Stedman Cottage, the administration building, Osborne Cottage, and a few shade trees were left standing.

The corner stones and memorial plaques salvaged from the old buildings were put into an Alumni Memorial erected on the new campus and dedicated at the annual reunion on June 13, 1971. To the 'old-timers' it was "a part of each of us, the last remaining symbol of physical things that enabled us to grow in wisdom and stature in childhood."[8] It was a reminder, too, of days when "the phrase 'I was raised at the Thompson

Old campus buildings fall to Third Street extension.

Orphanage' came to be an automatic recommendation for good character."[9]

NOT BETTER OR WORSE

For at least the first year after Thompson's move, people pointed with pride to the modern facilities and advantages of country living in the fresh air and rolling fields far from Charlotte's downtown traffic congestion. Others tearfully looked to the abandoned campus as an irretrievable memory, a ghost of happier days, and happier children. In reality, things were neither better nor worse at Thompson Children's Home; they were merely different.

Each of the new cottages was a family in miniature, with boys and girls of varying ages, and races, sharing both the responsibilities and privileges of family life under the guidance of full-time houseparents. With no fanfare or disruption, the first Black children had been admitted to the campus residence program in February, 1970. "We don't even see color any more," declared Robert Noble a few years later.[10]

Cottage life settled into a stable, family routine. The children had various duties they were expected to perform on a daily basis, and earned allowances of about three dollars a week for extra chores such as cutting the grass, cleaning the gym, or sweeping the front and back porches. They attended Sunday School and church at St. Martin's and had nightly devotions in the cottage. On Wednesday nights, the rector of St. Martin's joined them for prayers.

On school mornings, the children had to stir long before dawn, stumbling through the dark to catch their buses by 7:30 a.m. Senior high students went to Independence, juniors to Albemarle Road, 5th and 6th graders to Lincoln Heights, and elementary students to Idlewild. Weekends were filled with all types of recreational activities, from kick ball or basketball in the gym, to horseback riding lessons across the broad farm pastures. Swimming was extremely popular, although it was not a year-round activity until 1978 when St. Paul's Church Foundation in Winston-Salem donated funds to heat and cover the pool. In the library-gameroom, children enjoyed quiet activities such as reading or checkers and practiced for campus plays.

There was still work to be done on the farm,

Robert Noble finds new cottages have plenty of space for play.

which was now close at hand. Farm manager Dorsey Adams supervised the tasks and provided the children with a curiosity in the flock of pigeons he kept on the property. Wide hay fields supplied food for the beef cattle, and back-breaking work for the boys who had to gather the grain into bales. There was produce to be harvested — green beans, corn, okra, berries, watermelon — which helped cut down on each cottage's grocery bill. Surplus commodities such as flour and butter came from government programs, but there was inevitably a long weekly shopping list, such as this one borrowed from houseparent Mary Borchardt in 1972: 20 pounds of potatoes, six chickens, eight dozen eggs, 15-20 pounds of sugar, 10-15 loaves of bread, and 3½ family size packages of fish sticks.[11]

Most of the houseparents kept strict discipline. "If there hadn't been that strict discipline, I wouldn't be where I am now," explained Kenneth Thomas, who lived first in Smith Cottage on the old campus under housemother Rose McDade, then in Williamson Cottage on the new campus with Mr. and Mrs. Donald Honeycutt and later with Gary and Mary Borchardt. "I formed my lifestyle and my standards around what I obtained at Thompson," he said.[13]

"NOT A JOB, IT'S LIFE"

By 1973 many of the houseparent couples had been replaced with child care workers serving either full or part-time as supervisors in the cottages. In recruiting these "special people", cottage life director Clyde McSwain looked for "a person with a lot of physical stamina and emotional strength, someone who can give and take, day and night."[14] Ideal workers were in their 20's and 30's, "stable, but still young enough to relate to children . . . Someone who has led a sheltered life will be overwhelmed with the background of the kids."[15]

Child care workers took on all the responsibilities of parenthood, with none of its rights. They were not to replace the role of parents in the children's lives, but rather provide treatment-oriented supervision. What the children needed, said a new female child care worker, was "just to know somebody cares. It takes a long time for them to believe."[16] Being a child care worker, she said was "not a job; it's life."[17]

Group living also extended beyond the Margaret Wallace Road location in group homes at Lowesville in Lincoln County and in Greensboro, in addition to the original one in Goldsboro. The home used in Lincoln County was donated by James Osborne Moore, trustee and attorney for the institution, whose great-uncle was the first Thompson Orphanage superintendent, Edwin Osborne.

"CHRISTMAS ISN'T MERRY"

The degree of difference between 'old' and 'new' during these years was seen most clearly not in the gulf between Fourth Street and Margaret Wallace Road, but in the lives of the children. It was brought sharply into focus beginning with the 1971 Christmas holidays when a headline across the local front section of the December 20 *Charlotte News* candidly announced, "For These Kids, Christmas Isn't Merry." It was a tough concept for many church members, friends and supporters to comprehend. There was no enormous tree with gifts piled underneath, no festive holiday meal with mince pie and oyster stuffing, no traditional campus worship service. The celebration was fragmented, like the lives of the children. "This is a time for a lot of our youngsters when they're really confronted with what they don't have and what other people do have," explained Robert Noble. What most of the children didn't have was a real home, at least not one they could go to for the holidays. For the first time in recent memory, all of the campus cottages remained open during the Christmas season to care for those children who had nowhere else to go.

The numbers of children needing specialized care continued to climb during the early years of the decade, placing even greater demands on the institution. In April, 1972, John Young Powell was added to the staff as director of Thompson Children's Home and Robert Noble assumed the title of executive director of the state-wide agency, Episcopal Child Care Services. Mary Wunder, as director of Planning with Families and Children, took on the responsibility of counseling with parents to reunite the family, in addition to her other casework and admissions duties. Dr. Douglas F. Powers joined the staff as part-time child psychiatrist and counselor. A white-haired, craggy-bearded man, Powers brought considerable experience to Thompson Children's Home, having headed the child psychiatry programs at Vanderbilt University and Medical College of Virginia, and was distinguished professor of education at the University of North Carolina at Charlotte.

CAMPUS SCHOOL OPENED

On October 2, 1972, a school for children with learning disabilities was opened on the Charlotte campus using volunteer teachers from local colleges. Classes were first held on the lower level of the gym but were later moved into the individual cottages. William Gorman, an Episcopal layman from Richmond, Virginia was hired in 1973 to direct the on-campus education program. He held a masters degree in special education from the University of Virginia and had worked at Virginia Treatment Center, a psychiatric facility for children affiliated with the Medical College of Virginia in Richmond.

A REVEALING STORY

During his first Christmas as director of Thompson Children's Home, John Powell saw the "hurts of childhood" revealed in the life of a boy named David. The child was the only one who did not go home for the holidays.

His mother had promised to come for the day as the court would not permit overnight visits. David was anxious. He rode his bike back and forth between our home and the circle at the entrance to our campus . . .

Finally he gave up hope. 'She ain't coming, I know!' We tried calling but there was no answer. David's assumption that his mother once again was drunk was confirmed as the day wore on.

While his child care worker made arrangements for them to go out to dinner, David asked if he could help me work on my car. We had replaced the tail pipe and were lowering the jack when the car slipped, and the fuel tank punctured as it hit a supporting block, spilling gasoline all over the drive . . .

'Christmas is messed up for both of us, ain't it,' David asked me. And as two kindred spirits, we comforted one another and celebrated our friendship. It was Christmas now.[18]

GROUP HOME, TREATMENT COTTAGE ADDED

In September, 1973, Episcopal Child Care Services opened a second group home in Greensboro, offering care for pre-delinquent and mildly emotionally disturbed children. Goals for each of the group homes were improvement of the child's self-image and academic performance, correction of anti-social behavior, creation of a stable home environment for treatment, and involvement of the child's family in the overall plan of care.

The first cottage set aside for treatment of emotionally disturbed children on the Charlotte campus was opened in March, 1975 to handle the steadily increasing number of children for whom residential group care was the most appropriate alternative: children who could not tolerate the conformities or closeness of family-like living in a group or foster home. The cottage, named in honor of the Rt. Rev. Thomas H. Wright, Bishop of the Diocese of East Carolina, was the former residence of the campus director, renovated to accommodate about 6 children. Improvements included converting the back porch into a bedroom, adding two baths, and later enclosing the garage as a play room. It was officially re-dedicated as a treatment cottage on February 22, 1974, with William Gorman as its director.

During 1974 all but ten of the children served on the campus of Thompson Children's Home were classified as 'emotionally disturbed.' These were children who were much more difficult to deal with because their problems were more severe. And the differences between this growing group of youngsters and those who were merely dependent began to deepen. "Some of the first children began to resent the attention the others were getting because their needs were so different . . . On one hand you had some kids driving agency cars for dates, while those in the treatment cottage needed constant attention," described Powell.[19]

"A LOGICAL PATTERN OF GROWTH"

With a caution by the Executive Committee "not to drift into new programs but carefully debate and plan for changes in policy or program,"[20] the Board appointed a special study committee in 1975 to examine the changing population at Thompson Children's Home. Members of that committee were Executive Committee chairman Richard V. Bray, vice chairman James O. Moore, treasurer Erwin Laxton, the Rev. Robin Johnson of Gastonia, Robert Noble, and Ashley Gale, assistant executive director of The Duke Endowment. For assistance, they turned to several consultants: Sanford Howie, executive director of the Episcopal Church Home for Children in York, S.C.; Albert E. Trieschman, executive director of Walker Home and School for Children in Needham, Mass.; Robert Coates, executive director of Leake and Watts Home for Children in Yonkers, N.Y.; John Boswell, MD, associate professor of psychiatry at the University of North Carolina School of Medicine and director of child psychiatric services; and Lenore Behar, associate director for children's services in the North Carolina Department of Mental Health.

In its statement of the problem the committee recognized, "only a limited number of dependent and neglected children are being referred for group residential placement, while over 30 child care programs are competing for these more normal, easy to care for children."[21]

The current population of the Thompson campus is predominantly one that needs in-

Bishop Wright Treatment Cottage

tensive individual treatment, planned therapeutic group living and special educational help. County Departments of Social Services that represent our primary sources of referral have expressed a willingness to increase support costs sufficiently to make it possible for the Thompson campus to strengthen its program to a treatment stance. For these reasons we are recommending specific program changes.[22]

Those changes, presented to the Board as an 81-page document in January, 1976, included:

(1) Convert two additional cottages for residential treatment similar to that in Bishop Wright Cottage.

(2) Limit admissions to children ages 6-12 whose emotional disturbance is diagnosed as being reversible in the program of Thompson Children's Home, and whose treatment would not require longer than two years of residence on campus.

(3) Consider converting the remaining two cottages to treatment cottages.

(4) Continue serving children in family counseling or in the programs of group homes or foster family care.

(5) Adequately prove the agency's ability to finance the proposed programs.[23]

The researchers pointed out that it would be unwise for Episcopal Child Care Services to continue to compete with other agencies for the dwindling number of children without emotional handicaps. "We feel that this is not a new direction but a logical pattern of growth to meet the changing needs of children and their families in the name of our Lord."[24]

WHERE HAVE THE ORPHANS GONE?

The changing needs, and changing nature of the children in care were discussed by Robert Noble in March, 1976, in response to the question, "Then what in the world happened to the orphans?"

'Well, medical science happened for one thing. Parents are living longer. Fewer women are dying in childbirth. The economy changed, too. Since 1935, Social Security and other assistance has made it financially possible for relatives to care for children.'

Interviewer: 'Then, why should Thompson continue to operate? Why not close up? Isn't the job being done by other agencies?'

Noble: 'By and large, orphanages were established to meet a great need, the care of orphans. In most cases that need has been met. But the basic reason, meeting need, still exists. Families are in trouble. Many young people are coming into care emotionally disturbed, angry, and frightened by the problems of the family. Many parents are bewildered, unable to cope, and need help. Great need still exists! That's why Thompson now helps families to work through problems and get back together. Instead of *being* parents, we are helping parents to cope. The need changed. The program changed to meet the new need.'[25]

As to why Episcopal Child Care Services, and the church, had taken on such a difficult task, Noble responded, "We have no moral or theological basis for looking for the easy job . . . We are the Church in action. When we quit being pioneers, we ought to quit, period!"[26]

The Home's ability to finance its proposed expansion into a treatment facility for emotionally disturbed children was a very real concern. In 1975, income had exceeded expenses by just $22.66 and was the first year since the move to the new campus that there was no budget deficit. Several transactions over the previous few years had helped brighten the financial picture somewhat, chief among them being a resolution by the Diocesan Convention of North Carolina in 1973, which guaranteed that the agency would continue to benefit from the remaining ten acres of land formerly occupied by the old orphanage regardless of its use. The Rouse Company, developers of the Charlottetown Mall on 50 acres of orphanage land, held a conditional option on the property.

ST. MARY'S CHAPEL PRESERVATION

Those ten acres, and most especially the boarded-up St. Mary's Chapel, had been the subject of much public debate since the orphanage moved out in 1969. Even before the bulldozers left their mark on the old orphanage, there was concern that the chapel, spared from the Third Street right-of-way, continue to be preserved. Former orphanage residents Davis Poole and Ben Nash were among the hundreds of alumni who wanted to save the tiny chapel, as was former superintendent M.D. Whisnant. "I've been hoping some way would be found to preserve it," he said. "Too many children's lives—from the cradle right on through—are inside that little chapel."[27] Davis Poole, who rode by the chapel each day on his way to work, remembered 15 years of singing in the choir and listening to the old pump organ compete with the chirping birds outside.[28] For Ben Nash, who lived at the orphanage for 12 years, the chapel held memories of his wedding in 1935 and several years later, his son's baptism.[29] "The average person just doesn't realize what things like that mean to children with no homes," said Whisnant.[30]

A committee of interested citizens banded together to preserve and find new uses for the chapel. It was headed by Edwin Clarkson, grandson of the orphanage's first superintendent, and included Mrs. B.F. Withers, Mrs. John Glover, John Payne, William Sumner, John B. London, and Mrs. Charles D. Lucas who had donated land for the road at the new Thompson Children's Home campus. A variety of ideas were proposed, including one by City Councilman Jerry Tuttle that the chapel be dismantled and reassembled elsewhere. With the help of the Charlotte-Mecklenburg Historical

Commission, St. Mary's Chapel was designated an Historical Site by city-county ordinance in January, 1975. The designation stipulated that the building could not be altered or demolished without 90 days' prior notice by the owners.

When the Rouse Company chose not to exercise its option on the remaining portion of orphanage land in 1975, the Executive Committee of Episcopal Child Care Services agreed the best alternative was to sell the property which included St. Mary's Chapel. While recognizing its historic and emotional significance, the Committee members explained, "neither the Trustees of the Diocese of North Carolina nor the Executive Committee is empowered to preserve a historical building."[31] Speaking for the Committee, Robert Noble stated that the responsibility of the agency "is the care of children and the money from the sale of this property will make it possible to extend the Home's program."[32]

The interests of historic preservation and Episcopal Child Care Services were realized with the acquisition of 3.5 acres of the property by the City of Charlotte for a park. "The City Council has felt for some time that the property would make a nice park, and we would be able to preserve the chapel as well," stated assistant city attorney William Watts in a *Charlotte News* interview, October 3, 1975. The condemnation proceedings went to Superior Court to settle the purchase price, and at the November 10, 1975 meeting of the Executive Committee, treasurer Erwin Laxton reported receipt of a check for $428,135.13 from the City, which was forwarded to the trustees of the Diocese of North Carolina for investment. Thompson Children's Home would receive the annual interest on the money.

Another check was also received at that meeting, for $352,692.85 from the North Carolina State Employees' Credit Union, which had purchased the last 2.98 acres of the property bounded by Third Street and Kings Drive for an office building. On the site was the burned out skeleton of the administration building which had been set ablaze by arsonists in 1971, and finally met its ignominious end in October, 1975 as the Charlotte Nature Museum's "Haunted House.' These funds, too, would be invested by the Diocese of North Carolina with interest going to

Thompson Children's Home for operating expenses.

Again, the agency faced the dilemma of appearing to be rich. In truth, state and federal sources of funding were threatening severe cutbacks, voluntary giving was down, and there was a pencil-slim margin between revenue and expense in the operating budget. Selected appeals were made across the state, in addition to the annual Thanksgiving Offering, and the Episcopal Churchwomen were encouraged to continue their support as patrons and sponsors for specific needs rather than for individual children or cottages: needs such as food, clothing, child care workers' salaries, summer camp fees, and allowances. The Col. Edwin A. Osborne Society was organized in December, 1975 to recognize those who contributed $1,000 or more, with James Osborne Moore as its first president.

Plans proceeded for refurnishing St. Mary's Chapel and using it for cultural, educational, recreational, and religious purposes under the direction of the Mint Museum as agent for the City of Charlotte. Clean-up and restoration began in November, 1975 at a cost of $67,000.[33] At the April 16, 1976 meeting of the Executive Committee, Robert Noble reported on assurances from the Mint Museum that the chapel "will not be used for rock concerts or for political purposes." The old chapel had not been used for anything since 1969 except a wedding.

NOSTALGIC WEDDING LINKS PAST AND FUTURE

That wedding in 1974 was for the daughter of former orphanage resident Mary Froebe Penny. Although the sign on the door of St. Mary's Chapel threatened 'No Trespassing,' the bride and her mother were determined to have the building re-opened. With Robert Noble's permission, the family unboarded the windows, unlocked the doors and began cleaning. They found that transients had broken in through the basement and used the chapel as a shelter, warming themselves at a fire built in the center of the wooden floor. A charred circle still remained as evidence.[34] Undismayed, they scrubbed the floors and pews (with only the glow from a flashlight to mark their progress),[35] mowed the grass and clipped back the overgrown shrubs. They even got electricity, for the day, as a courtesy from Duke Power Company.

On June 15, 1974 the old black pump organ wheezed out the strains of "Here Comes the Bride' as Priscilla Lynn Penny became Mrs. Lester Wiley Burnette in the presence of 75 wedding guests in the Chapel of St. Mary.[36] That night, the bride's parents returned to again board over the windows and lock the doors.

The chapel wasn't opened for visitors again until August 29, 1976, when, after renovations by the City of Charlotte were completed, it was officially dedicated as an extension facility of the Mint Museum. A 75-pound cast iron bell, used during Charlotte's Bicentennial celebration, was hoisted into the steeple for the event which also included chapel tours, musical selections on the pump organ, and a bring-your-own picnic under the willow oaks which once sheltered the Thompson Orphanage.[37] The facility was dedicated as 'St. Mary's Chapel', shortened from the original 'Chapel of St. Mary the Virgin' in light of its deconsecration several years earlier. Uses planned for the chapel included art classes, a film series, chamber music performances, and weddings.

MEMORIES OF ROCK-FIGHTING DAYS

State senator Fred Alexander, an outspoken proponent of the chapel's preservation while on the City Council, was present for the ceremonies, declaring, "Back in my day, I could never come here — because I'm black. Now the little black boy from Brooklyn ends up preserving it for posterity."[38] He obviously enjoyed the twist history had taken since his earlier days of rock fighting with orphanage boys.

> Sugar Creek was the boundary line. Black children from Brooklyn would gather on one side, white children from Thompson Orphanage on the other, fighting with rocks. 'You know how it was in those days . . . the battles. Sometimes we'd win, sometimes they'd win.'
> . . . R.S. Fort, 74, remembered the fighting, too, from the years from 1913 to 1917 when he lived at the orphanage after his father died. 'That was more important than going

to school,' Fort recalled. Fort's recollection is the group that got to the creek first won the battle that day. He also remembers 'hollering out' big reeds and learning to fling rocks with them.[39]

The only thing missing from the chapel at the dedication was the old wooden cross, toppled from its roof-top perch a few months earlier during a violent thunderstorm. It had been rescued by Bob Noble and John Powell, who had stopped by the old campus to check on the storm damage, and was stored in the basement of the new administration building awaiting a fitting moment to be re-discovered.[40]

St. Mary's Chapel remained in the news after a skirmish erupted over placement of two contemporary sculptures in the adjoining Thompson Park. The first was a bulky piece of geometric aluminum entitled 'Kanturk,' placed near the chapel by the Mint Museum in May, 1977. The other was an unnamed work referred to as "the pole sculpture," placed on the grounds in October, 1980. The Charlotte City Council voted in February, 1982 to have the poles dismantled, and later Intech Corporation of Charlotte adopted 'Kanturk' for the front lawn of its offices.

EXPECTATION AND FAREWELL

The absence of a chapel on the new campus of Thompson Children's Home meant much less continuity in the spiritual training of the children. At first all the children had attended services at St. Martin's Church, but later each cottage attended a different Episcopal congregation in Charlotte. Executive Committee members agreed in March, 1977, that as more emotionally disturbed children came to the Home, religious activities would have to be centered on campus. They began carving out a job description for a campus chaplain, and planning for a new chapel.

In August, 1977, the group home in Goldsboro suspended operation for a period of re-examination into its operation and purposes. But both the study of the Goldsboro home and the proposal concerning a chaplain met an unexpected obstacle on October 29, 1977 with announcement of Robert Noble's intended resignation.

"Robert Noble decided if he stayed five more years as director of Thompson Orphanage, he'd probably never leave," explained a *Charlotte Observer* article on October 25, 1977. Noble had decided to take up a totally unrelated vocation, as a partner in a sailboat marina in Savannah, Georgia. "It's sad, too. I'm going to be leaving everything I know and everything I've been professionally trained for," he said. "It's been a super 16 years, really. We've come a long way, but I'm ready for new challenges."[41]

The agency's progress under Robert Noble was praised in a *Charlotte News* editorial:

> The Thompson Orphanage that Bob Noble joined in 1961 as assistant director was a model of the church orphanage, and a respected institution in Charlotte. But it was also an institution at the end of an era. It did not seek, and really was not equipped to handle, problem children. Its service was focused on the child, on campus. It was located downtown, next to Charlotte's largest black ghetto, but housed only white children. Change was recommended. It has fallen to Bob Noble to make those changes over the past 16 years. . . . What resulted was Episcopal Child Care Services, a highly professional agency increasingly devoted to providing specialized service and treatment to children and their families. . . . But the job has been done, in no small part because of Bob Noble's vision and skills. He has had a gift for recruiting quality staff. And a gift as well for drawing on precisely the right kind of outside advice required, whether the question is the future direction of the program, or the role of religion in a church-related professional treatment agency. Because of that, the agency he leaves behind is strong, well-staffed and very much believed in.[42]

A search committee was immediately appointed to find a new executive director. It was headed by Erwin Laxton, with James O. Moore and the Rev. Frank Vest, chairman of the Executive Committee. As applications for the position mounted and the date set for Noble to join his new venture neared, the committee asked that there be interim supervision of the agency until a new director could be found. John Powell, director of the Thompson Children's Home, and Robert Hawks, development director, were selected as interim managers.

In his parting remarks to the Executive Committee, Robert Noble urged special attention in the areas of finance, organization of the agency, and future plans. Specifically, he cautioned against too much reliance on government funds suggesting instead that other sources of giving be thoroughly pursued. And he said "it would be a mistake to hold off action on such matters as the Chaplain or the Goldsboro situation . . ."[43]

The Goldsboro home was re-opened in March, 1978 with a renewed commitment to provide general group care for school-aged children and their families, in particular dependent and neglected children who could be in care for an extended period of time, and those coming out of residential care at the Thompson Children's Home but whose families were not yet ready for their return. By August of that year, five children were living in the Goldsboro home. Selection of a chaplain, however, was delayed until 1981.

The capacity of the campus in Charlotte was, on recommendation of various consultants, reduced from 48 to 36, to better serve the intensive educational and psychiatric needs of the children. Even with its reduced capacity, Thompson Children's Home provided in 1978, over ten per cent of the total number of beds available to emotionally disturbed children in North Carolina.[44]

JOHN POWELL NEW EXECUTIVE DIRECTOR

After considering over 60 applicants, the search committee announced on June 12, 1978 its recommendation of John Y. Powell to be executive director of Episcopal Child Care Services, a recommendation unanimously approved by the Executive Committee and Board of Managers.

John Powell was originally employed by the Thompson Children's Home in 1972 to help meet the needs of the many more troubled children being admitted into the program. Through his training and skill, coupled with a gentle, soft-spoken manner, he had earned a place of trust in the hearts of children unused to trusting anyone. His background included a masters degree in social work, with specific concentration in psychiatric social work with children, from the University of North Carolina. He had

John Powell always has time for a child.

worked previously at the Episcopal Church Home for Children in York, S.C. and as director of Hillside Cottages treatment center in Atlanta.

Under his direction, the program at Thompson Children's Home had gradually evolved between 1972 and 1978 into a treatment center for troubled and emotionally disturbed youngsters. "It had been shades of grey all along," he emphasized. "We just kept getting more and more children with problems . . ."[45]

Between 1975 and 1976 the houseparents had been phased out. "These people just couldn't hold out all day, five days a week," Powell explained, "There was just more effort needed than (they) could give."[46] Replacing them were child care workers who rotated their supervision on shifts in order to give each cottage 24-hour coverage. Special education classes were expanded to serve all the children on campus who could not attend public school. Some thoughts had been given to enlarging the campus beyond its five cottages, but as Powell explained, "expansion made sense in the case of neglected children, but it was more difficult with emotionally disturbed children. It was really a question of how many disturbed children can you put in one spot" and still adequately serve their needs?[47] By 1979 Kenan and Christ Church cottages were converted to treatment cottages, making the agency's transition to a treatment facility complete. At the decade's end, nearly 15 per cent of all residential care, public or private, for elementary-aged children in North Carolina, was provided by Thompson Children's Home.

LILLIE MAE CLOSES OUT AN ERA

Another chapter in the agency's history was turned in October, 1978 when Lillie Mae White announced her retirement after 47 years as cook, laundress, housekeeper, dietician and friend to the children and staff of what would always be known to her as Thompson Orphanage. There was a big celebration of "Lillie Mae White Day" on October 16, 1976, which began at St. Mary's Chapel and moved to the present campus where Lillie Mae was treated to the first important Thompson meal she didn't have to prepare herself. " . . . I've worked long and hard enough," she vowed in a newspaper interview.[48] But she couldn't really stay away. Lillie Mae White continued to serve the agency part-time,

Lillie Mae White

preparing weekly lunches for staff meetings and meals for the Executive Committee and Board of Managers. Her second retirement was effective September 30, 1978 and this time she meant it.

The Home she left in 1978 bore almost no resemblance to the orphanage where she began work in 1929. It had a different name and a new location, with services spread across the state. There were no more dances in the kitchen or 'charity meat,' no more cows or dairy, and no orphans. Yet there remained important links to the past which were reassurance that the Episcopal church in North Carolina was continuing to fulfill its mission to serve children and families in need, no matter how those needs had changed.

FOOTNOTES

1. Dot Jackson, "Chapel Is Left To Its Wildwood — But For How Long?," *The Charlotte Observer,* April 7, 1970, p. 1B.

2. Dedication Poster, May 15-16, 1970, Thompson Orphanage Historical Files, Charlotte, N.C.

3. Sally Smith, "Children Will Host The Ceremony At The New Thompson Orphanage," *The Charlotte News,* May 13, 1970, p. 11A.

4. Dot Jackson, "Thompson Orphans Celebrate New Home," *The Charlotte Observer,* May 17, 1970, p. 25A.

5. Ibid.

6. Sally Smith, p. 11A.

7. Dot Jackson, "Thompson Orphans Celebrate," p. 25A.

8. Ibid., p. 2.

9. "Whoosh! they went, but the Corner Stones were saved," *Thompson Orphanage Alumni Association Newsletter,* June, 1971, p. 1.

10. Marilyn Mather, "Blacks, Whites Recall 'Battles' As They Dedicate Old Chapel," *The Charlotte Observer,* August 30, 1976, p. 2B.

11. Edith Low, "Their House Is Full Of Children And Love," *The Charlotte News,* September 21, 1972, p. 20A.

12. Kenneth Thomas, interview, April 6, 1985.

13. Ibid.

14. Janice Smith, "A Special Person," *The Charlotte News,* October 14, 1976, p. 1D.

15. Ibid.

16. Janice Smith, "They Found Their Niche," *The Charlotte News,* October 14, 1976, p. 1D.

17. Ibid.

18. John Y. Powell, "Healing the hurts of childhood," *The Communicant,* November, 1981, p. 6.

19. John Powell, interview, March 21, 1985.

20. "Minutes," Executive Committee, March 24, 1975.

21. "Report of Program Study Committee to Board of Managers," January, 1976, p. 1.

22. Ibid.

23. Ibid., p. 5.

24. Ibid., p. 14.

25. "Where'd The Orphans Go?," *The Charlotte News,* March 30, 1976, p. 1B.

26. Ibid.

27. Susan Jetton, "Cold Claws Of Progress Scratch At Chapel Door," *The Charlotte Observer,* April 28, 1973, p. 1B.

28. Ibid.

29. Ibid.

30. Ibid.

31. "Minutes," Executive Committee, April 21, 1975.

32. Ibid.

33. *St. Mary's Chapel — Thompson Park,* Charlotte Parks and Recreation Department, p. 3.

34. Mary Froebe, interview, March 16, 1985.

35. Claudia Newton, "Love, Happiness Fill Abandoned Chapel," *The Charlotte News,* June 18, 1974, p. 4A.

36. Ibid.

37. "Bicentennial Bell Will Ring For Chapel Opening," *The Charlotte News,* August 28, 1976, p. 6A.

38. Marilyn Mather, p. 1B.

39. Ibid., pp. 1B, 2B.

40. John Powell, interview, March 21, 1985.

41. "Orphanage Director Resigning," *The Charlotte Observer,* October 25, 1977, p. 6B.

42. "Bob Noble: a vision for children," *The Charlotte News,* October 26, 1977, p. 16A.

43. "Minutes," Executive Committee, January 31, 1978, p. 3.

44. "Minutes," Executive Committee, June 12, 1978, p. 1.

45. John Powell, interview, March 21, 1985.

46. Ibid.

47. Ibid.

48. Kays Gary, "Her 'Children' Never Forget," p. 1B.

Chapter 10

Tough Love

1980 — Present

Normally crowded on Sunday afternoons, the parking lots surrounding Outlet Square were straining capacity on October 28, 1984 as hundreds of curious shoppers surged into the shopping mall. Most had come looking for discount prices, many just for the fun of the celebration, and a few, for a glimpse into history 25 years past. It was the 25th anniversary of the shopping center originally known as the Charlottetown Mall.

Outside, the signal lights high above Independence Boulevard swayed and bobbed as traffic roared through the intersection at Kings Drive. At the crest of the hill across from Outlet Square, where once the Thompson Orphanage barn stood, Cinemas I-IV beckoned movie-goers to a crazy-quilt selection of features including "A Soldier's Story", "Buckaroo Banzai", "Body Double", and "Teachers." Behind the theaters, the wrap-around glass of the North Carolina State Credit Union building, set squarely on the spot of the old Thompson Orphanage administration building, sparkled in the afternoon sun.

Just below the cinema complex, where cows used to graze contentedly, aproned employees at "Wendy's" and "Shoney's" were cleaning up

from the after-church crowd, awaiting a new rush of customers spilling out from the movies. And just beyond the restaurants, where corn and hay once flourished on the Thompson Orphanage farm, a broad intersection beckoned travelers to the John Belk Freeway link to Interstate-77.

On the other side of Independence, the framework of a new housing complex pointed to the revitalization of the Cherry community. Only the Pearl Street Park, once a part of the original orphanage property, remained untouched.

The highlight of the anniversary celebration came at 3 p.m. when the tattered contents of the time capsule buried at the Charlottetown Mall in October, 1959, were displayed tantalizingly beyond reach in a glass enclosed case. Visitors jostled for position and craned their necks to get a peek. There were some pale photographs of mall construction progress, fragile editions of the **Charlotte Observer** *and* **Charlotte News,** *and assorted papers predicting the life and growth of Charlotte and the Piedmont in 1984.*

Few visitors stopped long enough to read any of the materials. Most gave a dutiful glance and shrugged as they filed by, pulled along by children anxious for other, more exciting treats: a cone of frozen tofutti or a bright mylar balloon emblazoned with the face of Papa Smurf. Still, a question hung in the air, voiced by a handful of passersby who knew or had heard that here was once a home for orphans — "Whatever happened to the Thompson Orphanage?"

Episcopal Child Care Services emerged into the 1980's as a progressive state-wide family and child social service agency facing imminent cutbacks in government support funds and explosive challenges created by the intensity of emotional problems brought to the program by the children and families in care. Through its reaction to these forces, the agency also had its greatest opportunity to show the church as a relevant, caring, healing force in an increasingly impersonal society.

In its statement of philosophy, Episcopal Child Care Services underscored its commitment:

> As a Christian agency we work to make such concepts as love, forgiveness, hope and redemption real in the lives of the children and their families. As a part of the ... process, Episcopal Child Care Services helps families to reach the conviction that they can, as a family unit, grow and learn to deal more effectively with their problems ... Basic to this philosophy is the Christian conviction of the integrity of the family as the fundamental social unit of society.[1]

The agency's scope of services in 1980 included the residential treatment center in Charlotte known as Thompson Children's Home, community group homes, foster family homes, and counseling services for families within their own communities.

REFUGEES FROM AN ANGRY WORLD

In a February 1980 article in *The Communicant,* newsletter of the Episcopal Diocese of North Carolina, the Thompson Children's Home, still the most dominant component of the agency's program, was described as "a cheery, modern refugee camp that offers its 36 children refuge from a world they cannot live in and families they cannot cope with. It is a place where healing can begin."[2]

... Thompson Home shows few signs of ten years' wear and tear but some things do need continual replacement — new mattresses are often needed because many of the children are bedwetters; drapery rods must be replaced because drapes are often the first target of abuse by an angry child. And anger is a common emotion among the children who live at the Thompson Home.

Where does the anger come from? Each child has a different story ... These children, damaged by the sickness of their families, experience behavioral problems as they get older. They cannot live in their families or function in society. Often they fail in school, despite average or above average intelligence. They are young refugees from today's world.[3]

The cover of the same church newspaper in November, 1981 succinctly explained the work of Thompson Children's Home in its headline, "Children Repaired."

John Oakes, a cottage supervisor, was convinced that Thompson Children's Home provided these refugees "the best individual care of children in the state,"[4] pointing to improvement in about 90 per cent of those in care and the fact that most were able to return to their own homes and families. But that care was increasingly expensive to provide, costing about $20,000 per child per year.[5]

GOVERNMENT FUNDS REDUCED

Government funds used to help finance this care had begun to dwindle in 1978, and by 1981 some sources had virtually disappeared. "Massive reductions in federal spending for social programs have especially hurt child welfare services," explained John Powell in a special report to the Board and Executive Committee in September, 1981. During the year, the budget was reduced by almost $200,000, the number of children served at Thompson Children's Home cut by ten with the closing of Christ Church Cottage until late summer, and the one remaining Greensboro group home was changed into a foster home center to help reduce operating costs.

Although Thompson Children's Home had maintained its expected revenue in custody-support payments through the first two months of the 1982 fiscal year, it was certain the trend could not continue because the counties which provided payments through federal Title XX funds were already out of money. "We are now exploring other sources of funding," explained Powell, "that will supplement our budget so that it can remain balanced."[6] He was particularly eager that Episcopal Child Care Services find sources of funds outside of government monies, so that it could maintain its integrity as a private, church agency. "If we were controlled by government funds, could we disagree with public policy?" he asked.[7]

CHAPEL BRINGS SENSE OF BELONGING

Consistent with its desire to remain identified with the church, Thompson Children's Home had sought to revive its spiritual roots since leaving the old campus and Chapel of St. Mary behind in 1969. The Home had been without a chaplain or a worship center for nearly 12 years.

The practice of sending the children to services at local Episcopal churches had been all but abandoned since, because of their severe emotional and social problems, they could not sit still or concentrate for long periods of time. Finally, in January, 1981, the Rev. Robin Johnson, rector of All Saint's Church in Gastonia and a member of the Board of Managers, was appointed Chaplain for Thompson Children's Home, and a gift of $150,000 was given by Roby Ellis Taylor and his son John Anderson Taylor of Winston-Salem for construction of a chapel on the Charlotte campus.

Interpreting Roby Taylor's desire for the chapel to be beautiful, comfortable and in a style the children could enjoy, architect James Hemphill suggested a country design of natural stone. Construction of the chapel began in October, 1981 and was completed in May, 1982. Officially dedicated as 'The Chapel of the Holy

The Chapel of the Holy Family defines the present campus. Adjacent is the administrative building.

Family' on May 27, 1982, the structure gave "a form and physical substance to the ministry of the Spirit which has always been present."[8] Chaplain Robin Johnson emphasized the significance of the new chapel:

> The structure of a building and corporate worship enhance not only the religious feelings, but also the self-discipline of a child. That is what helped our children remain in the chapel for the entire hour-long consecration service in which they participated both individually and collectively — a real feat for them. It was possible, not only due to the presence of staff, but to the environment of worship ... That idea would be impossible for them to articulate, but these children of fractured relationships knew they belonged there, in that place and at that time, as God's children, in His house, and as members of His family.[9]

The childrens' newly-emerging sense of family heritage was further solidified when the old cross which had fallen from St. Mary's Chapel in 1976, was retrieved from its basement storage and placed in the side hallway connecting the new Chapel of the Holy Family to the campus administration building.

Bishop Thomas A. Fraser, chairman of the Board of Managers, retired as Bishop of the Diocese of North Carolina at the end of 1982, satisfied that the Chapel of the Holy Family had helped put into perspective the continued role of the church in the programs of Episcopal Child Care Services. "Churches everywhere must learn to reach out to the hungry, the cold, the lost," he said. "Not just with Scripture, but with hands-on help as well. The Church has the greatest opportunity today that it's had in many a year. The question is, will we rise to it?"[10]

ADOPTION PREPARATION PROGRAM

As if in answer to Bishop Fraser's challenge, Thompson Children's Home progressed into yet another era by setting aside the Bishop Wright Cottage on January 20, 1984, as the stepping-out place for older children released for adoption. In an article on the Adoption Preparation Program, John Powell and Dr. Douglas Powers, the Home's child psychiatrist and counselor, explained:

Chaplain Robin Johnson (right) greets a visitor outside the Chapel.

Working with older, troubled children who may be adopted is nothing new in such agencies. However, in the long-overdue attempt to stay the merry-go-round of multiple, unending placements for children, more concentrated and refined therapeutic efforts frequently are necessary; and the residential treatment center is a highly desirable setting for a concentrated effort at helping certain children prepare for adoption.[11]

Not coincidentally, the clinical social workers on campus, under the guidance of Dr. Douglas Powers as editor, compiled their experiences with adoption of older children into a book. *Adoption for Troubled Children*, which was released just a few months after establishing the program in Bishop Wright Cottage.

In his report to the Board of Managers in September, 1984, John Powell confirmed the value of residential treatment at Thompson Children's Home, and the newly-inaugurated adoption preparation program:

> Recently a social worker from Guilford County wrote us about [a child] who recently left the Bishop Wright Adoption Preparation Cottage — 'As you know, I have been in close touch with your agency ... for the past two years regarding our work with this child who is being placed for adoption. I would like to take this opportunity to express my appreciation for the excellent work you have done

with him. I would never have dreamed that he would have come so far in 20 years, much less in two years!' ''

HEALING WORK QUIETLY CONTINUES

Amid the festivities of Outlet Square Shopping Center's twenty-fifth anniversary October 28, 1984, the link between the founding of the commercial complex in 1959 as Charlottetown Mall and the lease of its land from the Thompson Orphanage was nearly ignored, indicative in many ways of the quiet, unobstrusive manner in which Thompson Children's Home conducts its specialized programs today.

Far from the congestion surrounding Outlet Square, eight miles east past an endless string of discount chain stores, carpet outlets, fast-food restaurants, drive-thru banks, shoe stores and car dealerships along Independence Boulevard, the Thompson Children's Home sits nearly hidden off Margaret Wallace Road at St. Peter's Lane. Beyond its heavily wooded entrance is a secluded cluster of unpretentious buildings where, except for when snow covers the ground, boys and girls on bicycles are part of the permanent scenery.

The symbolic center of campus is the small, rough stone chapel connected to the administration building whose lobby resembles the front of a family refrigerator, greeting visitors with bright construction-paper drawings, and photos of children's snaggle-toothed smiles. Five cottages, which look like typical brick homes in any residential neighborhood, form the center of treatment activity. Four still bear old, familiar names: Williamson, Smith, Christ Church, and Kenan. The gymnasium and adjacent swimming pool provide organized, therapeutic recreation and opportunities for free play. A new access road connects the campus buildings and extends into the old farmland so that the lake can once again be used for recreation.

Between Kenan and Christ Church cottages is the Alumni Memorial encasing the cornerstones from the old Thompson Orphanage buildings and the now silent bell once called 'Old Faithful.' The raised letters encircling the bell are still legible: "For in thee the fatherless findeth mercy. Hosea XIV, iii."

The farm is gone, although down the road the old potato storage house and shell of the farmer's house are barely visible. Between the campus and the old farm is the Pheasant Knoll community, developed on acres of land purchased by contract option from Episcopal Child Care Services in 1983 and 1984.

Here in this pastoral retreat is the nucleus of the child-caring agency which has as its roots the Thompson Orphanage and Training Institution. Today its programs include residential treatment for emotionally disturbed children ages six to 12, extensive state-wide counseling services, and a community group home in Goldsboro. These services were combined in April, 1985 under the simpler, more recognizable title of 'Thompson Children's Home' although its official, legal name remains 'Thompson Orphanage and Training Institution' as stipulated in its charter.

Thompson Children's Home continues to be governed by a 22-member Board of Managers which includes the Bishops of the three North Carolina dioceses, three honorary members representing Episcopal Churchwomen from each of the dioceses and the remainder elected by the Conventions of their respective dioceses. Members serve staggered six, four or two year terms. The 15-member Executive Committee, elected by the Board of Managers, oversees the day-to-day operation of the agency.

THE THERAPEUTIC MILIEU

The residential treatment program in Charlotte is one of only three such services in North Carolina today. Its primary design is to assist children and families in identifying and resolving their problems, whether academic, emotional or social. Children placed in Thompson Children's Home are referred by county social service departments, juvenile courts, clergymen of all faiths, and often by their own families. Costs for providing each child's care range from $60 to $100 per day.

The treatment staff includes a pediatric psychiatrist as medical consultant, child care workers, special education teachers, therapeutic recreation leaders, registered pediatric nurse, family counselors and individual psycho-thera-

Behind the administrative building, sloping lawns lead to the treatment cottages.

pists.[12] The essence of the treatment approach is called a therapeutic milieu, "a special encompassing environment where disturbed children can mend deviant behavior, build self-esteem, improve academic performance and develop improved means of relating to peers and adults."[13] Every activity has a related therapeutic goal. Cottage chores teach responsibility and illustrate the functioning of a family. Games and team sports instill trust and confidence and chapel services reinforce a concept of worth and of belonging. Certificates and awards for the smallest school achievements help improve academic performance and stimulate self-confidence. No accomplishments go unnoticed or unrewarded, nor do eruptions of anger, aggression or defiance go unheeded. Regarded as cries for help, they are met with unqualified patience, skill, and love.

COAXED INTO LOVE

The stress on love, unearned and usually un-deserved, is equated by director John Powell with an infant's maturation within the family unit:

> The mother's task is to coax the baby into a love affair with her. Later the father and other family members will also elicit the infant's love. The healthy infant thus learns that love is not limited but actually increases the more one learns to love others. It is from such a foundation, I believe, that we learn to love God . . . We, of course, cannot repeat the infant-and-mother experience. But we can coax the hurt child into falling in love with some of us and support that relationship. In such a way, a new birth is possible . . . "[14]

Children are coaxed into 'new birth' through a campus culture which stresses improvement and achievement most visible in cottage assignment. When they are admitted, children are first assigned to a cottage where counseling and supervision are most intense. Some eventually move into the Bishop Wright Adoption Preparation Cottage which is a smaller unit with more similarity to family living. "Children respond favorably and with enthusiasm to this kind of deliberate planning . . . even though the cottage to which they are moving may not be a hundred yards distant," explains Dr. Douglas Powers.[15] The average stay on the Charlotte campus is between one and two years. Children leaving the residential program, either to return to their own homes, foster care, or a new adoptive home, receive extensive follow-up counseling and support, as do their families.

A coaxing into love is also the guiding principle behind the other components of Thompson Children's Home services. The foremost of these is preservation of the family through counseling. Counselors' primary efforts are in helping families evaluate and assess their own strengths, needs and goals. Then, if separation is necessary, care is taken to select the most appropriate setting, either in residential care or a group or foster home. Many children with special needs, particularly those in their early to mid-teens, find the attention they need in the community setting of the group home. Often the group home or a foster home is a second step for children coming out of residential care who are not quite ready to go home or whose families are not yet ready for their return. Thompson Children's Home does not operate its own foster family homes but places children in foster care through other public and private sources. Sometimes the best choice for a family is not any of these and referrals are made elsewhere.

IS IT WORTH THE EFFORT?

Plans are under discussion to help satisfy the unmet needs of other families in crisis with special programs for mildly retarded children and for troubled pre-teens and young teenagers if sufficient funds are available. Today, government funds account for only 25 per cent of the revenue budget, with trust funds and earned income providing about one-half of the revenue and another 25 per cent from annual voluntary giving. There appears to be no end to the needs of families and children but under the staggering weight of increased costs for care, scarcity of funds and the intensity of performance required of every staff member, the agency has asked itself, 'is it really worth it?'

After a particularly difficult meeting of the Board of Managers and Executive Committee in January, 1984 where justification for the agency's existence was closely examined, the Rev. Robert Ladehoff, then secretary of the Board who is now Bishop Coadjutor of the Episcopal Diocese of Oregon, affirmed, "We have no choice — we must help." Nowhere else, he said, could the "haven of tough love" be found: "love that cannot be broken, love that endures no

Love is a precious commodity.

132

matter what."[16] In a speech during the agency's Open House in November, 1984, Ladehoff again praised the unique quality of love which characterizes the program of Thompson Children's Home:

> Now, the love we are talking about here is a very special kind of love. It's not the soft, sentimental stuff you see in the movies. It's tough love: love that demands the best of a child, love that cannot be broken by anything the child could ever do: demanding, forgiving, enabling love: love that many of the children have never experienced before . . . It's never been so hard to make that love real. We're dealing with children who are neither loving nor loveable . . . We see what a great opportunity we have to introduce into a child's life a dimension of love he has never known before. It is an exciting and challenging time for us all.[17]

The measure of success for the programs of Thompson Children's Home is impossible to quantify. "For some emotionally-scarred children, just one day of simply being a child is a day of success," explains Brenda Lea, coordinator of financial development. "And it could be enough to turn a child's life around."[18]

ONE HUNDRED YEARS OF LOVE-GIVING

The Thompson Children's Home, direct descendant of the Thompson Orphanage and Training Institution, will enter its second century of service in 1986, caring for children whose basic need is the same as it was for the first orphans admitted to the institution in 1887. While these earlier children were orphaned by the death of their parents, children served in more recent years have been orphaned by the behavior of their parents. The void in their lives, however, has been the same: a need for love, not in the abstract, but love acted out through people. Remembering her days at Thompson Orphanage, Mary Froebe described the feeling of security she felt as the result of "love, and knowing who loves you."[19] Though much has changed since she left the orphanage in 1955, the security given by love has remained constant.

The staff of Thompson Children's Home is uniquely qualified to meet the need, realizing that "children don't care how much we know until they know how much we care."[20]

Throughout its one hundred years, the institution has carried proudly the name of Thompson, and in considerable measure has reflected the character of the man for whom it was named. In their 'Tribute to Lewis Thompson' in February, 1868, the members of the Bertie County Court predicted,

> His name will live for many years in the hearts of our people. Though his intelligent eye is closed in death, we fancy that it is still beaming upon us.[21]

FOOTNOTES

1. "Episcopal Child Care Services Philosohy," p. 1, Thompson Orphanage Historical Files, Charlotte, N.C.

2. Judy Lane, "Healing begins at the Thompson Home," *The Communicant,* February, 1980, p. 2.

3. Ibid.

4. Ibid.

5. Ibid.

6. John Powell, "Report to the Board and Executive Committee," September 25, 1981, p. 4.

7. Ibid., p. 5.

8. Robin Johnson, "ECCS Chaplain Talks About Chapel," *Talk 'n Tattle,* June, 1982, p. 1.

9. Ibid.

10. Kathleen Galligher, "Retiring Bishop Reflects On Career In Episcopal Diocese," *The Charlotte News,* February 8, 1982, p. 2B.

11. Douglas F. Powers, MD and John Y. Powell, "An Adoptive Preparation Program: Using Residential Treatment To Help Troubled Adoptable Children," *Residential Group Care,* Summer, 1984, pp. 7-8.

12. Powers and Powell, p. 9.

13. Ibid., pp. 9-10.

14. Powell, "Healing the hurts of childhood," p. 6.

15. Powers and Powell, p. 10.

16. "Minutes," Board of Managers, January, 1985.

17. Robert Ladehoff, speech, November, 1985.

18. Brenda Lea, interview, April 4, 1985.

19. Mary Froebe, interview, March 16, 1985.

20. "Orphans and Orphanages — North Carolina," North Carolina Room Files, Charlotte-Mecklenburg Public Library, Charlotte, N.C.

21. Bertie County Court, "Tribute," February, 1868.

Epilogue

"As for you, continue in what you have learned . . . because you know from whom you learned it." II Timothy 3:14.

He studied his vantage point carefully before settling down, checking the angle of sun and shadow across the gently sloping roof of the chapel. Quickly he flattened his hand against the corner of the paper as it was fluffed by a soft passing breeze. He squinted, then scowled and stared, forming the picture first behind his eyes before finally touching the pencil to the drawing pad.

The artist knew he had been right about the little chapel the moment he saw it. Its rugged stone exterior, nearly hidden entranceway, and the long, narrow triptych of stained glass set in the back wall affirmed it's significance, as did the name, Chapel of The Holy Family.

As he worked, grey lines scratched across the drawing pad took on the simple rectangular shape of the chapel, its gently arching roof sheltering the harsh, irregular stonework, and the few, low shrubs hovering near the base, nestled between the uneven walls of the building and the widening expanse of concrete and asphalt in the sidewalk and roadway. Lowering his drawing pencil to its side, the young man modeled the granite juts and creases along the convoluted walls, the soft chiaroscuro blending in shadow its sharp and rugged edges.

He held the sketch at arm's length, tightening his lips in a satisfied smile. Then he flipped back the pages of the drawing pad to the sketch he'd done earlier in the day. It was of St. Mary's Chapel at the old downtown location of Thompson Orphanage.

The contrast was immediate, dramatic. He had captured St. Mary's stately charm and wildwoods aura, surrounded as it was both by giant willow oaks and traffic-clogged streets. With ease, he had recreated its inviting warmth, symbolized in the front porch and wooden cross standing sentry over the doorway. But when he began defining the wide, flat bricks laid in long, even rows the geometric symmetry had produced an opposite, unsettling feeling. He had heard some of the chapel's history, enough to remember that Thompson Orphanage used to be on the property and that now St. Mary's was used mainly for weddings. But what about the children who had played around these dark brick walls and had worshipped in the mellow light cast by the impressive stained glass windows? Where were they?

He had found the answer at Thompson Childrens' Home and he knew now why his first drawing seemed incomplete. As streams of late afternoon sun picked out the irregular edges of each rough stone in the Chapel of The Holy Family, the artist saw clearly that these jagged rocks represented the lives of hurting children, each protrusion clamoring for attention, yet fitted gently and lovingly into place within the solid structure.

The young man set his drawings side by side on the ground, soothing Victorian Gothic abutting a rustic country facade, then pushed them together into a single work. "There," he said to himself with a gratified sigh. "It's a good beginning."

Bibliography

PRIMARY SOURCES

Annual Reports. Thompson Orphanage and Training Institution. 1887-1984.

Bertie County Court. "Tribute to Lewis Thompson." Feb., 1868.

Broten, Alton M. "The Group Child Care Project — Confidential Report To The Superintendent And The Board of Managers." 1957.

Deed Books 5, 6, 91. Mecklenburg County Register of Deeds Office. Charlotte, N.C.

Edwin Anderson Penick Papers. Diocese Archives. Raleigh, N.C.

Hopkirk, Howard. "Report of Survey." 1960.

Journal of the Annual Convention of the Protestant Episcopal Church in the Diocese of North Carolina. 1886-1895.

Lewis Thompson Papers. Southern Historical Collection. University of North Carolina Library, Chapel Hill, N.C.

Minutes of and Reports to Board of Managers. Thompson Orphanage and Training Institution. 1886-1985.

Minutes of Executive Committee. Thompson Orphanage and Training Institution. 1886-1985.

Osborne, Edwin Augustus. Unpublished autobiography from the private papers of Francis O. Clarkson, Charlotte, N.C.

Semi-Centennial Jubilee. A collection of papers and pictures authorized to be preserved for reference. Compiled by Josephine Osborne. May 7, 1937.

Superintendent's Record Book. Thompson Orphanage and Training Institution. 1886-1898.

Thompson Orphanage Historical Files. Charlotte, N.C.

PERSONAL INTERVIEWS

Froebe, Mary (Penny). March 16, 1985.

Henson, Stella (Batson). April 27, 1985.

Lea, Brenda. April 4, 1985.

Nash, Ben. April 10, 1985.

Powell, George. April 8, 1985.

Powell, John Y. March 21, 1985.

Thomas, Kenneth. April 6, 1985.

White, Lillie Mae (Hart) March 9, 1985.

SECONDARY SOURCES

Advertisement. *The Western Democrat*, Feb. 18, 1868, p. 1.

Bell, John L., Jr. *Hard Times: Beginnings of the Great Depression in North Carolina, 1929-1933.* Raleigh: Division of Archives and History, North Carolina Department of Cultural Resources, 1982.

"Bicentennial Bell Will Ring For Chapel Opening." *The Charlotte News*, Aug. 28, 1976, p. 6A.

"Bob Noble: a vision for children." *The Charlotte News*, Oct. 26, 1977, p. 16A.

Burwell, Mrs. Louis. "Charitable and Humane Institutions." *The Charlotte News*, May 26, 1914, p. 14.

The Carolina Churchman. (Charlotte, N.C.) 1909-1927.

"Celebration Is Held At Orphans' Home." *The Charlotte Observer*, May 8, 1937, p. 1.

"The Charlotte Orphanage." *The Charlotte Chronicle*, July 9, 1886, p. 1.

Charlotte Parks & Recreation Department. *St. Mary's Chapel — Thompson Park.* Pamphlet in St. Mary's Chapel.

Cheshire, Joseph Blount. *St. Mark's Church, Mecklenburg County, North Carolina — It's Beginnings: 1884-1886.* (n.p.)

_____ *St. Peter's Church, Charlotte, N.C., Historical Addresses From Colonial Days to 1893.* Charlotte: Observer Printing House, 1921.

_____ *The Church in the Confederate States.* New York: Longmans, Green, & Co., 1912.

Covington, Roy. "Orphanage Tract Is Leased For Huge Shopping Center." *The Charlotte Observer*, Nov. 23, 1954, p. 1B.

Duncan, Rev. Norvin C. *Pictorial History Of The Episcopal Church In North Carolina, 1701-1964.* Asheville: Miller Printing Co., 1965.

"Episcopalians Gather At Dinner Here Tonight." *The Charlotte Observer*, May 24, 1924, p. 6.

"Fanfare Opens Charlottetown Mall Today." *The Charlotte Observer*, October 28, 1959, p. 2C.

Fink, Arthur E. "Changing Philosophies and Practices in North Carolina Orphanages." *North Carolina Historical Review*, XLVIII, No. 4. Raleigh: Division of Archives and History, North Carolina Department of Cultural Affairs, Oct., 1971.

Galligher, Kathleen. "Retiring Bishop Reflects On Career In Episcopal Diocese." *The Charlotte News,* Feb. 8, 1982, p. 2B.

Gary, Kays. "Her 'Children' Never Forget Lillie Mae." *The Charlotte Observer,* Oct. 10, 1976, p. 1B.

Gray, Carole. "Houseparents Dispense Love With Discipline." *The Charlotte News,* April 12, 1969, p. 14A.

Greenwood, Janette T. *On the Home Front: Charlotte During the Civil War.* Charlotte: Mint Museum, 1982.

Hendrix, Jean. "Growth and Progress of Churches in Charlotte." *The Charlotte Observer,* Jan. 21, 1940, sec. 3, p. 9.

"Inspired Churchwomen Respond To Child Care Financial Crisis." *Talk 'N Tattle.* Winter, 1969, p. 2.

Jackson, Dot. "Chapel Is Left To Its Wildwood — But For How Long?" *The Charlotte Observer,* April 7, 1970, p. 1B.

——— "Stone Hid Past's Relics." *The Charlotte Observer,* June 3, 1970, p. 1B.

——— "Thompson Orphans Celebrate New Home." *The Charlotte Observer,* May 17, 1970, p. 25A.

Jetton, Susan. "Cold Claws Of Progress Scratch At Chapel Door." *The Charlotte Observer,* April 28, 1973, p. 1B.

Johnson, Guion Griffis. *Ante-Bellum North Carolina.* Chapel Hill: University of North Carolina Press, 1937.

Johnson, Robin. "ECCS Chaplain Talks About Chapel." *Talk 'N Tattle,* June, 1982, p. 1.

Kratt, Mary Norton. *Charlotte: Spirit of the New South.* Tulsa: Continental Heritage Press, 1980.

Kuralt, Charles. "Thompson Alumni Return." *The Charlotte News,* June 13, 1955, pp. 1B, 16B.

Ladehoff, Robert. Speech. Nov., 1985.

Lane, Judy. "Healing begins at the Thompson Home." *The Communicant,* Feb., 1980, p. 2.

Lefler, Hugh Talmage and Albert Ray Newsome. *The History of a Southern State — North Carolina.* 3rd. ed. Chapel Hill: University of North Carolina Press, 1973.

Liner, Edith Louise. *"Then Feed My Little Sheep."* (n.p.), 1976.

"Local Parishes Exceed Quotas." *The Charlotte Observer,* May 29, 1924, p. 2.

London, Lawrence Foushee. *Bishop Joseph Blount Cheshire, His Life and Work.* Chapel Hill: University of North Carolina Press, 1941.

Low, Edith. "Their House Is Full Of Children And Love." *The Charlotte News,* Sept. 21, 1972, p. 20A.

"Mall Opening To Be Today." *The Charlotte Observer,* Oct. 28, 1959, p. 1B.

Mather, Marilyn. "Blacks, Whites Recall 'Battles' As They Dedicate Old Chapel." *The Charlotte Observer,* Aug. 30, 1976, p. 2B.

The Messenger of Hope. Sept., 1894 and April, 1900.

Miller, Hannah. "Thompson Graduates Return To Orphanage For Reunion." *The Charlotte Observer,* June 25, 1962, p. 1B.

——— "Thompson Orphanage Heart Pounds With Love And Pride As Another Birthday Arrives." *The Charlotte Observer,* March 4, 1962, p. 1D.

Mizelle, Hazel. "Where Orphaned Children Get Loving Care." *The Charlotte Observer,* May 6, 1928, p. 5.

Munn, Porter. "Remember Queen City Cow Herd?" *The Charlotte Observer,* Oct. 28, 1959, p. 21C.

Newton, Claudia. "Love, Happiness Fill Abandoned Chapel." *The Charlotte News,* June 18, 1974, p. 4A.

"Orphanage Director Resigning." *The Charlotte Observer,* Oct. 23, 1977, p. 6B.

"Orphans and Orphanages — North Carolina." North Carolina Room Files. Charlotte-Mecklenburg Public Library, Charlotte, N.C.

Osborne, Clyde. "Theirs Is Push-Button Farm." *The Charlotte Observer,* Nov. 2, 1959, p. 4B.

Parramore, Thomas C. *Express Lanes and Country Roads: The Way We Lived In North Carolina, 1920-1970.* Chapel Hill: University of North Carolina Press, 1983.

Parramore, Thomas C. and Douglas C. Wilms. *North Carolina: The History of an American State.* Englewood Cliffs, N.J.: Prentice-Hall, Inc., 1983.

Powell, John Y. "Healing the hurts of childhood." *The Communicant,* Nov., 1981, p. 6.

Powers, Douglas F., MD and John Y. Powell. "An Adoptive Preparation Program: Using Residential Treatment To Help Troubled Adoptable Children." *Residential Group Care,* Summer, 1984, pp. 7-8.

"Raleigh Correspondence of the Democrat." *The Western Democrat,* Dec. 17, 1867, p. 2.

"Recent Developments at Thompson Orphanage." *The Mission Herald,* May, 1962, p. 6.

"Recognition Of The Independence Of Cuba." In *American Historical Documents.* The Harvard Classics. New York: P.F. Collier & Son Corp., 1938, pp. 440-441.

Romine, Dannye. *Mecklenburg: A Bicentennial Story.* Charlotte: Independence Square Associates, 1975.

Scheer, Julian. "Orphanage Not Cash-Heavy." *The Charlotte News,* Dec. 10, 1954, sec. 2, p. 1.

Simpson, Rita. "Orphanage Work Slated To Begin." *The Charlotte News,* Jan. 22, 1969, p. 2A.

Sitterson, Joseph Carlyle. "Lewis Thompson, A Carolinian And His Louisiana Plantation, 1848-1888: A Study In Absentee Ownership." In James Sprunt, *Studies In History and Political Science.* Vol. 31. Chapel Hill: University Of North Carolina Press, 1949.

Sketches of Church History in North Carolina — Addresses and Papers by Clergymen and Laymen of the Dioceses of North and East Carolina. Wilmington, N.C.: William I. DeRosset, Jr., 1892.

Smith, Janice. "A Special Person." *The Charlotte News,* Oct. 14, 1976, p. 1D.

——————— "They Found Their Niche." *The Charlotte News,* Oct. 14, 1976, p. 1D.

Smith, Sally. "Children Will Host The Ceremony At The New Thompson Orphanage." *The Charlotte News,* May 13, 1970, p. 11A.

Stellman, Joseph F. *North Carolina's Role in the Spanish-American War.* Raleigh: Division of Archives and History, North Carolina Department of Cultural Affairs, 1975.

Stone, Emily Whitehurst. "The Ties That Bind." *The Charlotte Observer,* Sept. 29, 1985, p. 7F.

Terrill, Tom E. and Jerrold Hirsch, eds. *Such as Us: Southern Voices of the Thirties.* Chapel Hill: University of North Carolina Press, 1978.

Thompkins, D.A. *History of Mecklenburg County and the City of Charlotte From 1740-1903.* Charlotte: Observer Printing House, 1903.

Thompson Orphanage Alumni Newsletter. 1954-1974.

"Thompson Orphanage: 'Built Through Love'." *The Charlotte News,* Feb. 24, 1962, p. 6B.

Trotter, Hazel M. "Thompson Orphanage Plans Extensive Business Section." *The Charlotte Observer,* Sept. 3, 1953, p. 1B.

Turner, Mary Anna. "A Fond Recollection." In *Saint Peter's Episcopal Church, 1834-1984 — A Fond Remembrance.* Charlotte, N.C. (n.p.), 1984.

Warren, Frank. "A New Concept In Care For Homeless." *Goldsboro News-Argus,* Nov. 1, 1964, p. 8.

Watson, Alan D. *Bertie County — A Brief History.* Raleigh: Division of Archives and History, North Carolina Department of Cultural Affairs, 1982.

"Where'd The Orphans Go?" *The Charlotte News,* March 30, 1976, p. 1B.

Zillman, Mamie. "Man, Nature Bless New Orphanage Site." *The Charlotte Observer,* Feb. 1, 1969, p. 1B.

Index